Less Stress = More Success

Teaching Relaxation and Stress Management to Kids

Grades Three Through Six

Susanna Palomares • Dianne Schilling

Cover design: Dave Cowan
Illustrations: Linda Thille

Copyright 2013, Innerchoice Publishing • All rights reserved

ISBN-10: 1-56499-088-4

ISBN-13: 978-1-56499-088-4

INNERCHOICE Publishing
15079 Oak Chase Court
Wellington, FL 33414

www.InnerchoicePublishing.com

Experience sheets may be reproduced in quantities sufficient for distribution to students in classrooms utilizing *Less Stress = More Success* activities. All other reproduction by any means or for any purpose whatsoever, is explicitly prohibited without written permission. Requests for permission should be directed to INNERCHOICE PUBLISHING.

DEDICATION

To Keith W. Ward, Ph.D.
with gratitude for numerous contributions to this book
and many seasons teaching stress management to educators

CONTENTS

YOUR INCREDIBLE BRAIN 9

LEARNING ENVIRONMENT 19

IDENTIFYING STRESSORS 29

RELAXATION 41

SUCCESS STRATEGIES 59

HIGH-STAKES TESTING 73

ANGER AND WORRY 83

EXERCISE AND NUTRITION 99

LESS STRESS = MORE SUCCESS!

INTRODUCTION FOR TEACHERS AND COUNSELORS

Stress is part of every student's life. An argument with a friend, moving to a new neighborhood, a family breakup, tests, grades, pressure from parents—the parade starts early and never stops. However, contrary to popular belief, stress doesn't come from the outside. The report card, the test, and the divorce are the stressors. The stress itself is in the person's response to those incidents. Stressors are the daily events that challenge an individual to adapt. Stress is the person's response as he or she attempts to make the adjustment, which is why the manifestations of stress are so variable from person to person.

Children benefit from some stress. Writing a report, preparing for an exam, rehearsing for a performance—all demand the stimulation of positive stress, which can help a student perform at his or her best. But stress can also be damaging. It can turn into distress. It can eat away at a student and consume so much energy that performance declines. Stress in the right proportions is a life enhancer. Excessive, prolonged stress is a life destroyer.

You will never eliminate stress from your classroom or counseling practice, nor should you. Stress management doesn't mean getting rid of all stress. It means helping children understand the stress response, identify individual and collective stressors, and learn and practice effective strategies for reducing stress and minimizing its destructive consequences. That in a nutshell is the purpose of this book.

UNDERSTANDING THE STRESS RESPONSE

Humans have inherited a physiological stress-response better suited to fending off attacking lions than coping with the stresses of modern life. During emergencies, a flood of hormones accelerates heart rate and breathing and rushes oxygen and nutrients to active muscles so that we can either defend ourselves against the perceived danger or beat a hasty retreat. At the same time, other bodily functions, including digestion, pain perception, and the immune system slow down or stop. The types of emergencies for which our ancestors evolved this "fight or flight" response were usually over quickly. Either they made it to safety or became somebody's dinner. In contrast, the stresses we face today, though rarely life threatening, tend to be recurring and persistent. School pressures, family squabbles, money worries, minor disagreements, tests, grading, and hundreds of other features of everyday life can produce the pounding headache, queasy stomach, racing heart, and sweaty palms we associate with stress. Furthermore, the stress response may kick in over and over again throughout a typical day.

The main stress hormones involved in the stress response are *epinephrine* (better known as *adrenaline*) and the steroid hormone *cortisol*. Epinephrine acts in seconds, while cortisol backs up epinephrine over minutes or hours. It's the longer acting cortisol that most often leads to health problems, as it tends to linger in the system long after the stressful event is over (which may explain why a person still agitated from one stressful encounter tends to react more easily to the next one). The brain activates the stress response whether a person actually experiences something stressful or just thinks about it.

EFFECTS ON HEALTH AND LEARNING

Stress compromises the immune system and increases vulnerability to viral infections such as the common cold. The scientific link between stress and colds is compelling—and just the tip of the iceberg. Stress triggers asthma attacks, raises blood pressure, exacerbates heart disease, contributes to ulcers and colitis, and worsens chronic pain. Furthermore, stress can short circuit memory, impede learning, and permanently damage the brain.

In **Brain Rules** (2008, p. 178), molecular biologist John Medina observes:

> Stressed people don't do math very well. They don't process language very efficiently. They have poorer memories, both short and long forms. Stressed individuals do not generalize or adapt old pieces of information to new scenarios as well as non-stressed individuals. They can't concentrate. In almost every way it can be tested, chronic stress hurts our ability to learn.

Memory and information are stored in neural networks—vast arrays of connected neurons. Learning and storing memories involves the strengthening of some branches rather than others in the network. Much of the action takes place in the cortex and the hippocampus of the brain, both vital to memory. In **Why Zebras Don't Get Ulcers** (1998), neuroscientist Robert Sapolsky uses this simple computer analogy to illustrate the relationship between the two: The cortex is like our hard drive, where memories are stored, and our hippocampus is the keyboard, the means by which we place and access memories in the cortex.

Sapolsky explains that short-term stress, if not too severe, can enhance memory by spurring glucose delivery to the brain and making more energy available to neurons. You may remember every detail of the circumstances surrounding your first kiss, or receiving news of the Challenger explosion, or the World Trade Center disaster. These are examples of short-term stress enhancing memory formation and retrieval.

There are dozens, probably hundreds of neurotransmitters that pass information across the synapses between neurons. The most important one in the cortex and hippocampus is glutamate. Glutamate works a little differently than other neurotransmitters. Instead of a small amount of glutamate causing a little bit of neural excitation (and, thus, a little bit of learning), a small amount often produces no effect at all (no learning). A little more glutamate, and still no response. A nonlinear threshold of excitation must be reached before learning is achieved. As that connection continues to be reinforced at the threshold level, eventually it is "potentiated," which means that the synapse has learned something.

Memory is disrupted when stress becomes too great or prolonged. Not only do learning and memories fail to occur, they may actually be depressed, so that we start forgetting things as well. Glucose delivery to the hippocampal areas of the brain subsides, too, so the brain gets less energy. Memory and concentration are seriously compromised during times of stress.

So just as a student is struggling to perform well on the SAT, the long-term potentiation and nourishment of hippocampal neurons are being reduced. With even more sustained stress, cortisol actually begins to damage neurons. With prolonged stress, axons and dendrites in neural networks begin to shrivel, atrophy, and retract. As the complexity of neural networks declines, so does the student's ability to access stored information. The memories may still be there, but it takes longer to retrieve them.

There is also growing evidence that severe stress may lead to the permanent loss of hippocampal neurons (Sapolsky, 2004). MRIs of people with post-traumatic stress disorder (PTSD), including victims of physical and sexual abuse and people with severe depression, have shown major and selective atrophy of the hippocampus. In many cases the tests were completed long after the trauma occurred, suggesting that the damage may be permanent.

Accelerated learning experts have recognized for decades that stress inhibits learning and have consistently promoted the use of relaxation exercises like visualization and music to reduce stress and increase energy levels prior to and during learning sessions (Jensen, 2000). More recently, the "mindfulness" movement has successfully advocated the routine use of breathing exercises, progressive relaxation, and a variety of classroom interventions to help manage student stress (Lantieri, 2008). These techniques help all children—especially the anxious ones—cope with stress more effectively.

SYMPTOMS AND COPING STRATEGIES

Most of us associate stress with the responsibilities of adulthood—going to work, paying the bills, keeping relationships on an even keel. We don't often realize that children and teens are subjected to many of the same stressors that gnaw at us, and perhaps a good many more that we know nothing about. Childhood is anything but carefree for kids whose families are dysfunctional or disintegrating, who are exposed to domestic violence, surrounded by gangs and drugs, spend hours alone while their parents work, or are poorly nourished, and emotionally neglected. And, as we know from our own lives traumatic events are by no means the only sources of stress. Social pressures, school performance, peer teasing and bullying, and over-scheduling by super-competitive parents can leave a young person exhausted.

Some children experience extremely high levels of performance anxiety. Every test is a crucible of their competence as a person. Excessive anxiety can interfere with attention and also with memory. When the stress reaches an intolerable threshold, some kids become phobic about school, often inventing illnesses and injuries in order to stay home.

In ***Building Emotional Intelligence*** (2008), author Linda Lantieri points out that symptoms of unmanaged stress in children are often mislabeled as inappropriate behavior requiring disciplinary action. Teachers and parents reprimand their children for actions that are really stress reactions, rather than intentional misbehavior. Signs of stress may include:

- Increased physical illness (headaches, stomachaches, chronic fatigue)
- Withdrawal from people and activities
- Anger and irritability
- Sadness, tearfulness
- Worry
- Nervousness
- Difficulty sleeping
- Difficulty concentrating

The 2008 national Kids Poll conducted by the Nemours Foundation in collaboration with Southern Illinois University and numerous health agencies and reported at KidsHealth.org asked children ages 9 to 13 what things caused them the most stress. Top categories were: grades, school, and homework (36 percent); family (32 percent); and friends, peers, gossip, and teasing (21 percent).

The same poll found that young people rely on a variety of coping strategies to handle stress. For example, 52 percent of kids reported playing or doing something active when stressed. Other popular strategies were listening to music (44 percent), watching TV or playing video games (42 percent), talking with a friend (30 percent), trying not to think about the problem (29 percent), trying to work things out (28 percent), and talking to a parent (22 percent). Potentially negative strategies included eating (26 percent), cutting, banging, or otherwise hurting themselves (25 percent), losing their temper (23 percent) and crying (11 percent).

AN ECLECTIC APPROACH TO STRESS MANAGEMENT

Activities that promote social-emotional learning (SEL) form an optimal foundation for school stress-reduction programs. Children who develop awareness of feelings, thoughts, and behaviors, who master their emotions, build effective communication and relationship skills, and learn to manage conflict are in a much stronger position to effectively cope with the perils of everyday stress. In the 1970s and 1980s, it was the affective education and self-esteem movements that led the way in teaching social-emotional skills. More recently, SEL has become a principal focus of the push to develop emotional intelligence and mindfulness in children. In his foreword to Linda Lantieri's (2008) book, **Building Emotional Intelligence**, Daniel Goleman equates SEL with "the systematic classroom teaching of emotional intelligence." He argues that helping children master their emotions and relationships makes them better learners.

This book approaches stress management broadly. Activities help children to understand the effects of stress on the brain, take steps to de-stress the learning environment, identify sources of stress, practice breathing and relaxation exercises, adopt habits that promote successful learning, understand the effects of nutrition and exercise on stress, and learn to more effectively manage anger and worry.

Getting children involved. Having a sense (or illusion) of control over one's circumstances has been shown to alleviate stress. This is a tough one for young people, because they don't often have the power or resources to take matters into their own hands. However, even very young children can participate in establishing classroom rules and procedures, building both a sense of control and the commitment necessary to ensure success. We've included several activities that involve children in creating a more stress-free learning environment by identifying ways to achieve a state of "relaxed alertness" throughout the school day.

You can further increase student involvement and sense of control by listening "actively" when children exhibit distress, by helping them label their emotions and build a feeling vocabulary, and by teaching them how to use problem-solving to resolve stressful issues and conflicts. Older children can be taught to change their reactions to stressful events, promoting a lower heart rate, deeper breathing, clearer thinking, and feelings of calmness and control. The student who fakes a sprained ankle in order to avoid a stressful school environment is exerting some degree of control over her situation, but needs to learn better ways of coping.

Recognizing stress. When stress is pervasive, it's tempting to conclude that chronic tension and anxiety are normal states while serenity is rare. Instead of a smooth road with an occasional bump, life becomes a rough road with an occasional rest stop. Before kids become habituated to stress, we need to help them distinguish between ordinary conditions and stressful ones, so that they know stress when they see and feel it. Therefore, several activities in this book are devoted to helping children recognize the physical, emotional, and behavioral signs of stress, identify individual sources of stress, and link emotional highs and lows to stressful events.

Learning to cope. The largest group of activities in the book is dedicated to helping children identify, evaluate, and practice various approaches to managing stress, including common coping strategies like those identified by the Kids Poll and several relaxation exercises. The children conduct interviews with adults and peers; experiment with humor and laughter; relax to music; and practice mindfulness through deep breathing, meditation, and progressive muscle relaxation.

The goal of mindfulness activities is to relax the body while focusing the mind. Systematic lessons and regular practice result in numerous benefits, including these five described by Lantieri (2008):

1. Increased self-awareness and self-understanding
2. Greater ability to relax the body and release physical tension
3. Improved concentration and ability to pay attention, which is critical to learning
4. Ability to deal with stressful situations more effectively
5. Greater control over thoughts, with less domination by unwelcome thoughts

A dose of prevention. One of the best ways to manage distress is to keep it from happening in the first place. By learning and practicing proven success strategies—life skills such as goal-setting and time management—children perform better in school and function more effectively in relationships. Acquiring life skills builds greater confidence, and greater confidence increases resilience in the face of all kinds of stressful events and circumstances. Several success strategies are addressed by activities in this book. Children learn to monitor their self-talk, use positive affirmations to reduce anxiety, set short and long-term goals, use time-management tools, and identify sources of help and support in the school, neighborhood, and community. In addition, several activities help children cope more effectively with the stress produced by high-stakes testing.

Managing anger. Anger is a common symptom of stress. Anger is also a stressful emotion, regardless of what triggers it. It is destructive to the health of the student who experiences it and, when expressed negatively or violently, to those on the receiving end as well. Furthermore, anger is a kind of default emotion, erupting swiftly when a young person's feelings are intense and confused but he or she lacks the ability to accurately label them. As children gain emotional intelligence, incidents of anger subside, in part because they learn to recognize and deal with the frustration, fear, embarrassment, jealousy, humiliation, and other feelings that so often precede anger. *Less Stress = More Success* includes activities designed to help children understand the potential health consequences of anger, identify symptoms and triggers of anger, complete self-monitoring logs, role play anger-inducing scenarios, and commit to anger-management strategies.

Health and fitness. Exercise is one of the most popular and effective ways of relieving stress and, like healthful eating, serves a protective function as well. Being physically fit builds endurance and helps children weather stressful conditions and maintain normal body weight. Activities in this book help children set fitness goals, make positive lifestyle choices, explore various forms of exercise, calculate their working heart-rate range, and increase flexibility through stretching. In addition, children study food pyramids and nutrition-facts labels, develop meal and snack menus, and examine personal eating habits.

REFERENCES

Jensen, E. (2000). *Learning smarter: The new science of teaching.* San Diego: The Brain Store.

Lantieri, L. (2008). *Building emotional intelligence: Techniques to cultivate inner strength in children.* Boulder, CO: Sounds True.

Medina, J. (2008). *Brain rules: 12 principles for surviving and thriving at work, home, and school.* Seattle: Pear Press.

Sapolsky, R. (2004). *Why zebras don't get ulcers: An updated guide to stress, stress-related diseases, and coping.* New York: W.H. Freeman

What kids say about: Handling stress. (2008). Retrieved Dec. 18, 2008, from http://kidshealth.org

USING THE ACTIVITIES

This book is designed to be used with children in third through sixth grades, so an occasional modification may be necessary to optimize the activities for your children. The level of difficulty among the activities also varies slightly. If you like an activity, but think that the presentation is too sophisticated for your children, look for ways to modify it. Simplify the vocabulary, revise the explanations, and give examples that your children will find familiar. Adjust the activities to suit the maturity, reading ability, cultural background, and interests of your children.

Many of the activities are accompanied by reproducible "experience sheets" for the children to complete in class or, in a few cases, as homework.

We've grouped the activities by topic area and arranged them in an order that makes sense to us, however most of the activities will stand alone and may be implemented in any order you choose. We recommend that you integrate the activities within your regular lesson plans, adding them wherever they seem appropriate. Once you've introduced the relaxation and breathing exercises, try to repeat them often, or substitute similar exercises from other sources. Make relaxation a regular part of the classroom and school routine.

Every activity includes a list of open-ended, thought-provoking discussion questions. These questions are a vital component of the activity. During discussion, children translate experiential learning into cognitive understanding and commit concepts to long-term memory. If you omit the discussion following an activity, you run the risk of weakening the experience. If the questions seem irrelevant based on what your children experienced while completing the activity, come up with new ones that build on the lessons they learned.

YOUR INCREDIBLE BRAIN

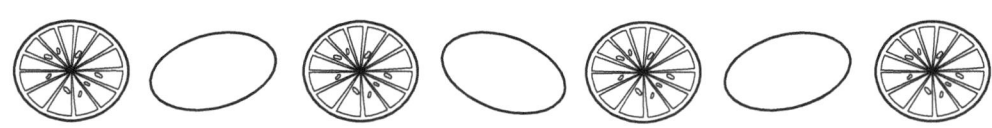

A THOUGHT EXPERIMENT

These first three activities are designed to illustrate the power of imagination to influence behavior. People are just as likely to react to imagined situations as to real ones, and this is why even situations that don't pose any real danger can still produce stress. By helping children understand this, and by helping them understand that they have the power to change their thoughts, they have more ability to manage stress.

OBJECTIVES   Children will:

- Experience the power of imagination to produce physical sensations.
- Describe how various thoughts produce emotional reactions.
- Recognize how thoughts alone can cause stress.

MATERIALS   None

DIRECTIONS   Tell the children that you are going to have them test the power of their imaginations. Ask them to sit relaxed at their desks with their hands on the desks and feet flat on the floor. Next, ask them to close their eyes and listen carefully as you slowly, with feeling and emphasis, read the following directions:

Imagine a bright yellow lemon sitting in front of you on your desk. Imagine that you are picking up the lemon. Feel it's rough skin. The lemon is full of juice and you can feel its weight. Now imagine that you have a sharp knife in one hand. With the other hand, hold the lemon steady as you safely cut the lemon in half. Notice the sour juice that drips out of the lemon and onto your desk. Smell the pungent odor of the juice. Pick up half of the lemon. Feel the juice dripping into the palm of your hand and running down your

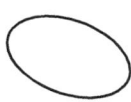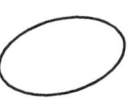

11

wrist. Lift the lemon to your nose and smell it. Now, take a big bite out of the lemon. (Pause) Open your eyes.

Ask the children to describe any feelings and sensations they experienced as they imagined holding, cutting, and eating the lemon. Typical responses are, "I had a sour taste in my mouth," "My jaw felt funny," and "My mouth watered."

Ask the children to explain how such reactions are possible, since there was never any lemon in the first place. Use their responses to spark a discussion about the power of imagination. Make these points:

- If your mouth watered at the thought of eating the lemon, your stomach probably secreted enzymes to neutralize the acid in the lemon juice. Your body may have reacted in other ways that you were unaware of, too.

- Your brain reacted to your thoughts about the lemon just as if the lemon were real. In the past, when you tasted a real lemon, your brain stored the memory of its flavor and your reaction. When you have experienced something and reacted in a certain way, just the thought of it can make you react in the same way again.

DISCUSSION QUESTIONS

1. *If you had never tasted a lemon, what do you think you would experience?*
1. *How do you react when someone tells a scary story?*
1. *What is something that you feel anxious just thinking about?*
1. *What is something that you feel embarrassed just thinking about?*
1. *What can you do to reduce the stress caused by imagined fears?*

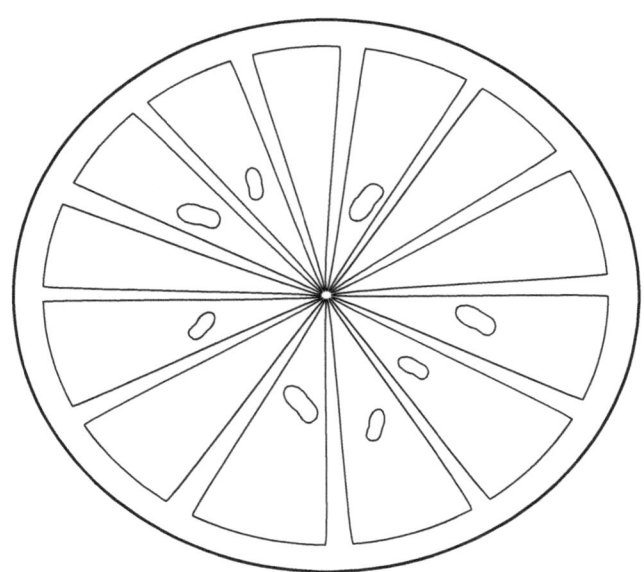

POSITIVE THOUGHTS VS. NEGATIVE THOUGHTS

OBJECTIVES   Children will:
- ❤ Recognize how thoughts affect feelings.
- ❤ Change negative thoughts to positive thoughts.
- ❤ Demonstrate how negative self-talk produces negative behavior, and positive self-talk produces positive behavior.

MATERIALS   None

DIRECTIONS   List the following words on the board:

Situation   Thought   Feeling   Behavior

Using the headings as a visual guide, explain to the children that in many situations, what they think and say about the situation heavily impacts how they feel about the situation and what they do (their behavior) as a result of the situation.

To illustrate this point, have the children close their eyes and listen carefully while you read the following situations, demonstrating the impact of contrasting reactions to the same event.

RAINED OUT

Response A

Situation: A trip to your favorite theme park is canceled because of heavy rain.
Thought: "That really sucks. The whole day is ruined. There's nothing to do."
Feeling: Angry, disappointed, miserable, bored
Behavior: Mope around. Talk sullenly to everyone. Accomplish little or nothing.

13

Response B

Situation: A trip to your favorite theme park is canceled because of heavy rain.
Thought: "We will go in good weather. Today's a great day to read."
Feeling: Optimistic, confident, creative, content
Behavior: Enjoy indoor activities. Talk pleasantly to others. Get a lot done.

A POP QUIZ

Response A

Situation: Your teacher surprises the class by giving an unannounced math quiz.
Thought: "I don't know this stuff. This isn't fair. I'm going to fail."
Feeling: Angry, pessimistic, low energy
Behavior: Complain. Get a slow start. Do poorly on the quiz.

Response B

Situation: Your teacher surprises the class by giving an unannounced math quiz.
Thought: "This will show me what I need to work on. I'll do the best I can."
Feeling: Accepting, determined, optimistic
Behavior: Pay attention. Focus on the questions. Pass the test.

Have the children open their eyes. Ask them: "How did thoughts affect feelings and actions in these examples?" Facilitate discussion, in the process making these points:

- Thoughts are easier to control than feelings.
- Since thoughts often produce feelings, many times we can change our feelings by changing our thoughts.
- When thoughts and feelings change, behavior usually changes, too.
- We are responsible for what we think, how we feel, and what we do.

Have the children form teams of four. Give each team one of the following situations (or other situations that you create). Explain that each team will create two short plays dramatizing their situation. The first play will demonstrate the effects of negative thoughts. The second will demonstrate the effects of positive thoughts. Urge the teams to refer to the headings on the board. Their job is to show how negative thoughts, and then positive thoughts, produce contrasting feelings and behaviors.

Situations
- Giving a speech to the class
- Attending a teacher conference with your parent
- Playing in a championship game
- Learning a new sport
- Not being invited to a party
- Doing homework

Have each group perform its contrasting plays, back-to-back, for the class. Facilitate discussion after each performance.

DISCUSSION QUESTIONS

1. *How did thoughts influence feelings in this play? How did they influence behavior?*
1. *Have you ever changed your feelings about something by changing your thoughts? Tell us what happened.*
1. *What is one negative thought that you often have that you could change?*
1. *How difficult is it to change your thoughts about something?*
1. *Who is responsible for your thoughts? What about your happiness?*

EXERCISE THE IMAGINATION WITH BRICKS AND BALLOONS

OBJECTIVES Children will:
- Experience the power of imagination to influence behaviors.
- Describe how thoughts produce feelings and behaviors.
- Understand the connection between imagination (thoughts) and stress levels.

MATERIALS None

DIRECTIONS Ask the children to stand and space themselves evenly around the room. Give them the following directions, while you demonstrate the process, checking to see that everyone's hands are correctly positioned:

Stretch your hands out in front of you at shoulder height. Turn the palm of your left hand so that it is facing up toward the ceiling. Turn the palm of your right hand so that it is facing toward the floor. Close your eyes. Keep your eyes closed and hold this position until I tell you to open your eyes.

Take a deep breath and relax. Imagine that your left hand is holding a very heavy, dark red brick. Feel its weight. Now, imagine a large, helium-filled balloon floating above you and tied to your right wrist with a string. Look up and see the brightly colored balloon. Feel it pulling against your wrist as it tries to rise to the ceiling. Feel the brick pressing down on your left hand, forcing it toward the floor. Notice the weight of the brick getting heavier and heavier in your left hand. Feel the string tugging lightly on your right wrist as the balloon attempts to rise higher. The balloon wants to rise. The brick wants to fall. The balloon is light. The brick is heavy. The balloon is pulling on your right hand, while the brick is pressing heavily on your left hand.

Tell the children to open their eyes and look around the room. Ask them what they notice. Most of the children will have moved their hands involuntarily during the experiment, lowering their left hand (the one with the brick) and lifting their right hand (the one with the balloon). Give the children a few moments to comment on what they observe. Then have them take their seats and discuss the results.

Emphasize the power of imagination to influence behavior, even in the absence of conscious awareness. The brain-body is just as likely to react to imagined conditions as it is to real conditions. The high incidence of imagined fears and anxieties makes this particularly relevant to stress management. Help children understand that by changing their thoughts, they can often change their feelings and bodily reactions, which in turn can reduce stress.

DISCUSSION QUESTIONS

1. *About how many inches did your hands move during the experiment?*
1. *What do you think caused your hands to move?*
1. *Were you aware that you were moving your arms and hands?*
1. *How did your left hand and arm—holding the brick—feel?*
1. *How did your right wrist and arm—holding the balloon—feel?*
1. *What did you learn about your imagination from this experiment?*

Adapted from an activity by Keith Ward, Ph.D.

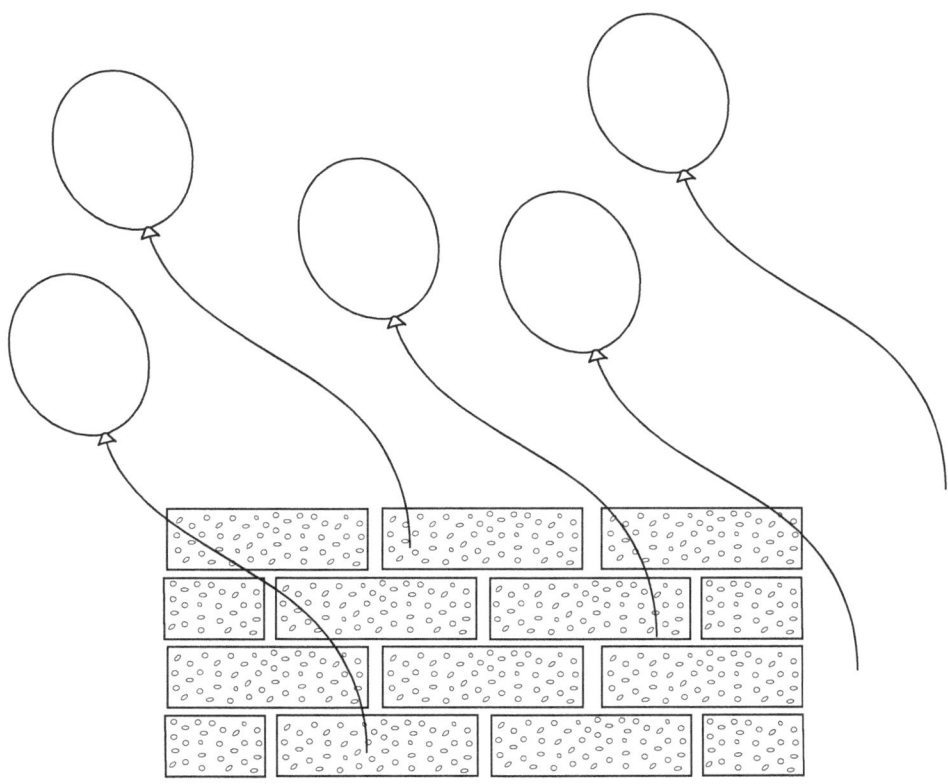

LEARNING ENVIRONMENT

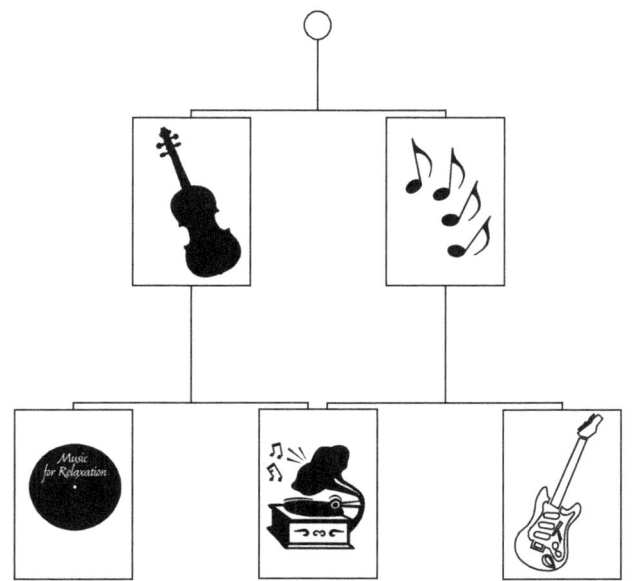

HOW RELAXED ALERTNESS (R-A) AFFECTS PERFORMANCE

People learn best and remember what the learn better when they feel both relaxed and alert. This activity is designed to help the children grasp the concept of relaxed alertness appropriate to their age and experience.

OBJECTIVES   Children will:

- Describe and compare feelings of relaxation and alertness.
- Identify situations in which they felt both relaxed and alert.
- Discuss benefits associated with relaxed alertness.

MATERIALS   Chart paper or white board, and markers

DIRECTIONS   Ask for a show of hands from children who feel relaxed "at this very moment." Call on two or three and ask, "How do you know that you are relaxed?" Encourage the children to describe the feelings and physical sensations that indicate relaxation, such as feeling calm, loose-limbed, peaceful, pleasant, and well.

Next, ask for a show of hands from children who are alert "at this very moment." Repeat the process, asking volunteers, "How do you know that you are alert?" Elicit feelings such as focused, aware, wide awake, and attentive. Throughout the discussion, help the children broaden their feeling-word vocabulary by suggesting and defining appropriate new words.

Explain to the children that people learn best and remember what they learn longer when they feel both relaxed and alert while they are learning. State in your own words at a level appropriate to the age and understanding of your children::

Feeling relaxed can open your mind. It can boost your curiosity and make you eager and interested. Feeling alert can help you pay attention and stay focused so that your senses —your eyes and ears — take in more information. Experiencing both at the same time sets the stage for optimal learning.

Continue the discussion until most of the children grasp the concept of relaxed alertness at a level appropriate to their age and experience. Then ask the children to close their eyes and recall a time when they felt both relaxed and alert. State:

Think of a time when you were totally relaxed and at ease and, at the same time, completely concentrated on the task at hand. You might have been completing a puzzle, drawing a picture, solving math problems, or shooting baskets. The task may have been difficult or easy, but because you were both relaxed and alert, it probably felt enjoyable and you made good progress. When you think of something, recall as much as you can about the incident and your feelings.

Ask several volunteers to share their experiences of relaxed alertness. As each volunteer briefly describes an incident, write key words on the board (or chart paper) under the heading "Situation." Then ask the volunteers how they know that they were both relaxed and alert in the situations. Record their comments in a second column under the heading "How I Know I Was Relaxed and Alert." Ask discussion questions (below) to help the children describe characteristics of the incidents, including outcomes, benefits and, especially, their feelings. Conclude the activity with a general discussion summarizing what the group learned about relaxed alertness.

DISCUSSION QUESTIONS

1. *What feelings or sensations did you have in your body during the incident you described?*
1. *What emotions did you experience?*
1. *How much time passed during the incident? Did it seem like a long time, or a short time?*
1. *What did you learn from the incident?*
1. *How much of what you learned do you remember today?*
1. *How did you feel about your performance in the situation? Was it a good job?*
1. *What does it take to feel both relaxed and alert in a situation? How can you make it happen more often?*
1. *What can we do to increase relaxation and alertness in our classroom?*

Adapted from an activity by Keith Ward, Ph.D.

DEVELOPING A PLAN FOR RELAXED ALERTNESS

This activity extends the learning about relaxed alertness introduced in the last activity. The Children offer their ideas for developing a plan to increase relaxed alertness in the classroom.

OBJECTIVES   Children will:
- Share ideas for increasing relaxed alertness in the classroom.
- Develop a plan for implementing relaxed-alertness strategies.

MATERIALS   One copy of the experience sheet "Bright Ideas for Relaxed Alertness" for each child; one copy of the summary sheet for each team of four; chart paper or white board, markers

DIRECTIONS   Remind the children of the previous activity highlighting the benefits of relaxed alertness. Tell them that you would like their help in developing a plan to increase relaxed alertness in the classroom so that everyone will not only feel better, but learn more easily and effectively. State:

All of us can contribute in some way. For example, everyone might feel more relaxed if study and reading periods were quieter, or if soft music were playing in the background. Alertness might increase if we all got at least eight hours of sleep every night, or if we worked in teams more often. There are many ways to increase relaxation and alertness. See how many ideas you can think of.

Distribute the experience sheets and go over the directions. Give the children a few minutes to individually complete the sheet.

Have the children form teams of three or four. Tell each group to select a recorder. Distribute summary sheets to the recorders. Instruct the groups to take turns sharing the ideas they wrote on their experience sheets. Have the recorders write all ideas on the summary sheet, eliminating duplications.

Encourage the teams to discuss the ideas on their lists, adding details and refinements.

When the teams have finished sharing (15 to 30 minutes), have the recorders take turns reading their lists to the entire group while you record ideas on the board or chart paper.

Go back over the final list and discuss individual items with the group. Eliminate items that are impossible to implement and circle items that are feasible and promising. See if you can get buy-in from the children on at least five items to try. If any of the five items requires an action plan, appoint a committee to work on it and set aside the necessary planning time. Note: Be sure to capture the final list on paper.

DISCUSSION QUESTIONS

1. *Which idea on the final list will be the most difficult to achieve? Why?*
1. *Which will be the easiest to achieve? Why?*
1. *How can we help each other stick to the plan and make it work?*
1. *How do you feel about coming to this classroom every day? How would you like to feel?*
1. *Who wins when we make our classroom a great place to learn?*

Adapted from an activity by Keith Ward, Ph.D.

BRIGHT IDEAS FOR RELAXED ALERTNESS
EXPERIENCE SHEET

You learn best when your mind and body feel relaxed — not tense, worried, or uptight. It also helps to be *alert* — wide awake, listening, and interested. Feeling both relaxed and alert at the same time is especially cool.

What can we all do to make the classroom a better place to learn? What things will help us feel relaxed and alert? Write three ideas here:

1. _____
2. _____
3. _____

What can you do to make the classroom a better place to learn? Do you need to change a behavior? Could you do more of something, or less of something? List three ideas here:

1. _____
2. _____
3. _____

Copyright © Innerchoice Publishing

 # SUMMARY SHEET

List your team's ideas for increasing relaxed alertness and making the classroom a better place to learn.

1. _____
2. _____
3. _____
4. _____
5. _____
6. _____
7. _____
8. _____
9. _____

List your team's ideas for things that individual children can do. Add a check mark to an idea each time it is suggested by a different child.

1. _____
2. _____
3. _____
4. _____
5. _____
6. _____
7. _____
8. _____
9. _____

CREATING A RELAXED ALERTNESS POSTER

> In this third activity of the series on relaxed alertness the children will reinforce and support the ideas they came up with for increasing relaxed alertness by creating posters for display.

OBJECTIVES   Children will:

- Create posters illustrating specific strategies for achieving relaxed alertness.
- Group the posters in a semi-permanent display.
- Demonstrate their commitment to the plan.

MATERIALS   The final list of ideas for increasing relaxed alertness in the classroom (from the previous activity); large sheets of poster board; construction paper in various colors, scissors, marking pens, glue, and miscellaneous decorative materials; computers and publishing software (if available)

DIRECTIONS   Display the final list of ideas for improving the learning environment through relaxed alertness (from the previous activity). If more than a few days have elapsed since the list was generated, spend a few minutes reviewing the concept and benefits of relaxed alertness.

Announce that the children will be working in small teams to create posters illustrating the agreed-upon strategies from the final list. When the posters are finished, another team will assemble them in a single display showing the entire plan. The semi-permanent display will remind and motivate everyone to stick to the plan. Note: If any of the teams will be creating computer-generated posters, arrange the logistics.

Have the children form teams of no more than three members each. Assign each team one of the ideas from the final list of strategies. Duplications are okay. Suggest that the teams take a few minutes to brainstorm words, pictures, symbols, and other graphics that convey their strategy. For example, "Sleep 8 Hours Every Night," could be illustrated with the face of a clock, a sleeping head on a pillow, a spiral of ZZZZZ's of different sizes and colors, and a poem or quotation about sleep. Some of the items could be drawn directly on the poster board, and others cut from colored construction paper, or illustrated on bold construction-paper shapes.

Distribute the art materials, or have the children select what they need from a central location. Teams that are using computers will want to review available clip art and photographs.

When the teams are ready, have them take turns sharing their finished products with the entire group. (This might need to occur in a follow-up session.)

Take a few minutes to brainstorm ideas for the final display. Encourage the children to think creatively. In addition to a bulletin-board display, think of ways to create a free-standing three dimensional display, or to group posters in mobile-like arrangements that can be hung from the ceiling. Choose three or four enthusiastic children to make the final decision and build the display.

DISCUSSION QUESTIONS

1. *Why is it helpful to be relaxed while you are learning?*
1. *How does being alert help you to learn?*
1. *How many of you were relaxed and alert while making your posters?*
1. *Can you be relaxed and angry at the same time? What about relaxed and scared?*
1. *How does being tired affect alertness? What about being hungry?*
1. *How can we help each other be more relaxed and alert, more of the time?*

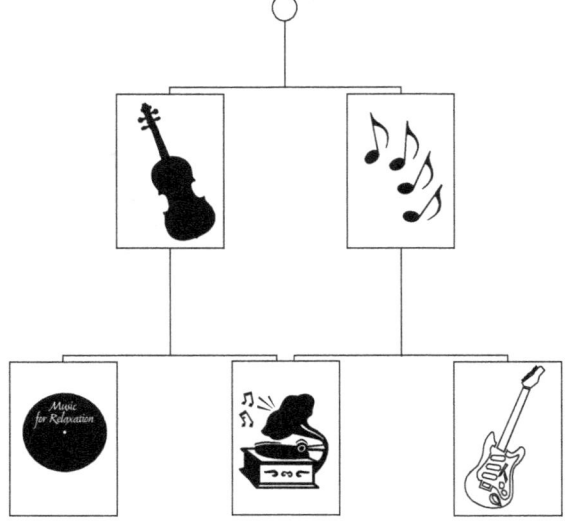

IDENTIFYING STRESSORS

RED-ORANGE

WHERE DO YOU FEEL YOUR STRESS

Stress can often have a strong physical effect. Everyone "feels" stress in their bodies, in their own way, but there is no denying that all bodies feel stress. This activity helps children recognize their own physical reactions to stress. When they are aware of these reactions and strategies for managing them (developed later in this book), they are better able to take action to lessen the stress and its negative effects.

OBJECTIVES Children will:
- Identify areas of the body where stress reactions occur.
- Represent those reactions with color in creative drawings.
- Use the drawings to describe how stress feels.

MATERIALS One copy of the experience sheet "The Color of Stress" for each child; crayons or colored marking pens

DIRECTIONS Remind the children of discussions the group has had about stress, particularly those dealing with the feelings and physical sensations associated with stress. Ask a few questions to spark a quick review. Then state:

Our bodies can react strongly to stressful situations. Sometimes we don't realize what is causing those reactions. For example, you might get a headache or feel a little queasy after having an argument with a friend, or after being late to school because you missed the bus. If the reaction occurs a couple of hours later, it's easy to overlook the cause. That's just one reason why it is important to understand how you usually respond to stress.

Distribute the experience sheets and the drawing materials. As you go over the directions, emphasize the use of color. Urge the children to choose colors that represent their feelings. For example, what color comes to mind when they imagine feeling irritable, nervous, excited, or scared? Encourage the children to be as creative as possible and remind them that they all react to stress, but each in a different way.

Ask volunteers to show their completed drawings to the rest of the class and talk about what each rendering suggests and represents.

DISCUSSION QUESTIONS

1. *What is the strongest reaction you have to stress?*
1. *What color did you use to represent that reaction?*
1. *What is the most unpleasant reaction you have to stress?*
1. *How did you represent that reaction?*
1. *Where in our bodies are strong and unpleasant reactions usually located?*
1. *What do you usually do when you have feelings like these?*

RED-ORANGE

THE COLOR OF STRESS
EXPERIENCE SHEET

Your body sends out signals when you experience stress. Sometimes the signals are very strong, such as when a loud crash makes you jump and your heart starts racing. Other times the signals are weak, such as when you feel a bit nervous before a quiz.

Use the picture of the body to mark the locations where you notice stress signals.

1. Draw an X on each part of the body where you feel stress. You may draw one X or several.

2. Think about how your body feels in each location you have marked.

3. Choose a different color to represent each feeling or sensation.

4. Use that color to fill in the area where the reaction occurs.

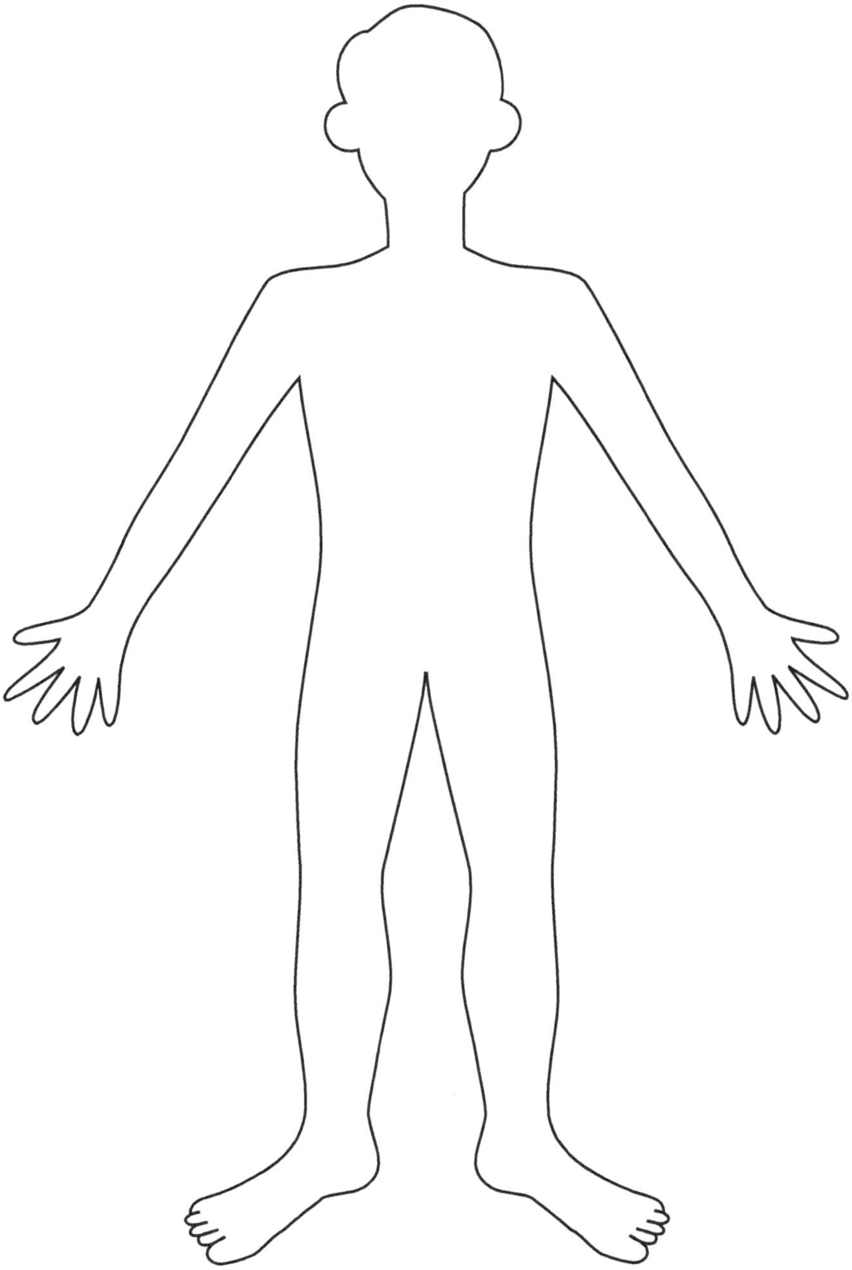

WHAT STRESSES YOU OUT?

> The first step to managing stress is to understand what causes our bodies to react in a flight or fight response. The first part of this activity helps the children to identify personal stressors through a self-assessment. This leads into a discussion about effective ways to relax and to get their minds off what is stressing them out. This allows their bodies to recover from the flight or fight response.

OBJECTIVES Children will:
- Describe the "fight or flight" response in their own words.
- Identify specific things that cause stress in their lives.
- Name activities that tend to reduce stress.

MATERIALS One copy of the experience sheet "What Stresses You Out?" for each child

DIRECTIONS Explain to the children that what we call stress, and the feelings that accompany stress, are not only natural and normal, they have been experienced by every human being who has ever lived. State:

Our earliest ancestors, the hunters and gatherers who lived long ago, evolved a very effective response to threats from predatory animals and other dangers. We call it the "fight or flight" response, because it helped them get ready to either stand their ground and fight an attacker, or try to escape. When your heart pounds and your muscles get tense, when your eyes widen and your fists clench, you are experiencing almost exactly the same physical response. But, instead of worrying about hungry lions, you worry about tests, and grades, and peer pressure, and a busy schedule that sometimes leaves you exhausted. Your bloodstream is flooded with the same chemical brew that helped your ancestors survive terrible threats to their safety, but you don't really need all those chemicals. In fact, they can end up damaging your health. That is why it is so important to learn to manage stress. When you know how to calm down and relax, you can slow or stop the flow of chemicals before they do any damage.

Point out that the first step to managing stress is to understand what causes the stress (fight or flight) response. Tell the children that they are going to complete a short self-assessment in order to identify sources of stress in their own lives.

Distribute the experience sheet, go over the directions, and allow time for completion. If you are working with lower-grade children, consider demonstrating the process. Allow about 10 minutes for completion.

Read through the stress factors listed on the experience sheet, asking for a show of hands from the children who marked each item. After polling an item, ask volunteers to elaborate on their individual experiences. Make notes on the board to keep track of the most common sources of stress.

Next, talk to the children about the need to take breaks when they feel stressed. Explain that a break is anything that helps them relax and gets their mind off tough issues. Ask the children to describe the stress breaks they listed on their experience sheets. Write their ideas on the board under the heading "Stress Breaks." Then brainstorm additional strategies, including:

- Jog or walk
- Listen to music
- Spend time with your pet
- Work on a hobby
- Play a game
- Browse the Internet
- Watch TV or a movie
- Practice a musical instrument
- Dance
- Play outdoors
- Talk with a relative or friend
- Make a plan to solve the stressful problem

Emphasize that stress breaks give the children time to recover from the fight-or-flight response, so that their bodies don't continue to produce potentially damaging chemicals, and that this is the primary goal of all stress-management strategies.

DISCUSSION QUESTIONS

1. *What is meant by the words fight-or-flight response?*
1. *What is the fight-or-flight response designed to accomplish?*
1. *Why is the same event stressful for one person, but not stressful for another?*
1. *What things do most of us in this group find stressful?*
1. *How does your body feel when you are stressed?*
1. *Why is it important to relieve stress? What can happen if we don't?*

WHERE DOES STRESS COME FROM?

 EXPERIENCE SHEET

Read the list below. Put a check mark (✓) beside any item that has happened to you. Put the check mark in the "B" column if the experience was bad. Put the check mark in the "G" column if the experience was good.

B	G	My stress comes from…
____	____	Trying to feel accepted
____	____	Arguing with my parents
____	____	Doing things I shouldn't because of peer pressure
____	____	Trying to make new friends
____	____	Worrying about my appearance
____	____	Feeling sad over the death of a pet
____	____	Feeling left out
____	____	Not having enough money
____	____	The death of a family member
____	____	Fighting with my brother or sister
____	____	My grade on a test
____	____	Arguing with or losing a friend
____	____	My ability in sports
____	____	Responsibilities or chores at home
____	____	Having no one to talk to
____	____	Death of a friend or classmate
____	____	Changing schools
____	____	Worrying about my safety
____	____	The separation or divorce of my parents
____	____	Grades on my report card
____	____	Thinking about vacation
____	____	Moving to a new neighborhood
____	____	Trying to please my parents

Take a Stress Break
Two things I do to feel better when I am stressed:

1. _____

2. _____

THE HEAVY WEIGHT OF STRESS

> This is another activity that helps children identify the stress they experience and learn about how it affects them. An important lesson from this activity is that positive events can also be stress producing. And, it's also important to learn strategies to manage positive stressful events as well as negative.

OBJECTIVES Children will:

- Understand stress and how it affects daily life.
- Describe how positive as well as negative events lead to stress.
- Identify individual stressors.

MATERIALS One copy of the experience sheet "Boulders in My Backpack" for each child

DIRECTIONS Spend a few minutes discussing the concept of stress — what it is, what it feels like, and how it interferes with daily life. State:

Stress is the general feeling of discomfort you experience when one or more responsibilities, problems, important events, worries, or life changes are weighing on your mind, demanding attention and energy. The things that cause stress are often referred to as stressors, and the more you are dealing with, the heavier the load. Imagine adding a rock to your backpack for every stressor in your day. Worried about a test? Add a rock. Have an argument with a friend? Add a rock. Big game this afternoon? Add a rock. Trouble with grades? Add a rock. Excited about a big event? Add a rock. Pretty soon it feels as though your backpack is bulging with boulders.

Ask the children to describe how stress makes them feel. As they share, write key words and phrases on the board. Common responses include: tense, tired, confused, drained, depressed, shaky, unable to concentrate, frustrated, exhausted, worthless.

Using age-appropriate vocabulary, paraphrase the following points about stress. Record notes on the board under these headings:

NEGATIVES

- Worrying about stress won't make it go away.
- You can't outsmart stress.
- Good things cause stress, too.
- Stress can lower your resistance to illness.

POSITIVES

- Understanding stress can help you manage it.
- You can learn to head off stress if you know where it comes from.
- Adequate rest and healthy eating can help you cope with stress.
- You can learn stress-reduction techniques.

Distribute the experience sheets and go over the directions. Give the children a few minutes to complete the sheet. When they have finished, go through the items with the entire group, asking for a show of hands to see how the items were rated. Ask volunteers to explain their ratings. Focus on both positive and negative feelings. Generate discussion throughout this process.

DISCUSSION QUESTIONS

1. *How does being excited about something cause stress?*
1. *How does wanting to perform well cause stress?*
1. *What did you learn from rating different stressors?*
1. *How will this information help you manage your own stress levels?*
1. *How does stress affect our classroom?*

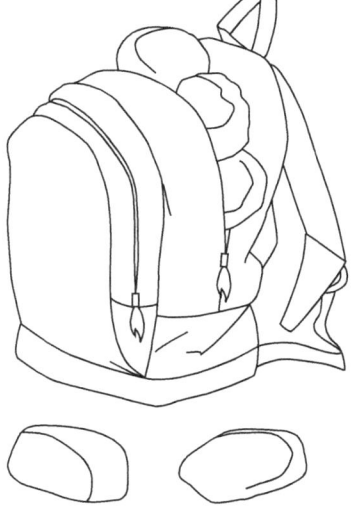

BOULDERS IN MY BACKPACK
EXPERIENCE SHEET

What if every stressor was represented by a rock in your backpack? The weight of all those rocks could get pretty heavy by the end of the day. Even if everything that happened was "good," some of it would still be stressful.

How you react determines whether something is stressful or not. For example, being called on in class is probably OK when you know the right answer, but it can be embarrassing when you don't. The excitement of being invited to a party can be just as stressful as the disappointment of not being invited. Decide how much stress you would feel in each of these situations. Put an X on the scale from 1 (no stress) to 5 (very stressful).

Not Stressful .... **Very Stressful**

1. Holding a snake .... 1 ___ 2 ___ 3 ___ 4 ___ 5 ___
2. A photo of a snake .... 1 ___ 2 ___ 3 ___ 4 ___ 5 ___
3. A school holiday .... 1 ___ 2 ___ 3 ___ 4 ___ 5 ___
4. Getting an A on a test .... 1 ___ 2 ___ 3 ___ 4 ___ 5 ___
5. Getting a D on your report card .... 1 ___ 2 ___ 3 ___ 4 ___ 5 ___
6. Math class .... 1 ___ 2 ___ 3 ___ 4 ___ 5 ___
7. Choosing teams in PE .... 1 ___ 2 ___ 3 ___ 4 ___ 5 ___
8. The first day of school .... 1 ___ 2 ___ 3 ___ 4 ___ 5 ___
9. The last day of school .... 1 ___ 2 ___ 3 ___ 4 ___ 5 ___
10. A surprise quiz .... 1 ___ 2 ___ 3 ___ 4 ___ 5 ___
11. Arguing with a friend .... 1 ___ 2 ___ 3 ___ 4 ___ 5 ___
12. Making a new friend .... 1 ___ 2 ___ 3 ___ 4 ___ 5 ___
13. Being late for school .... 1 ___ 2 ___ 3 ___ 4 ___ 5 ___
14. Test-taking .... 1 ___ 2 ___ 3 ___ 4 ___ 5 ___
15. Your birthday .... 1 ___ 2 ___ 3 ___ 4 ___ 5 ___
16. Strange noises in the night .... 1 ___ 2 ___ 3 ___ 4 ___ 5 ___
17. Being alone in the dark .... 1 ___ 2 ___ 3 ___ 4 ___ 5 ___
18. Recess .... 1 ___ 2 ___ 3 ___ 4 ___ 5 ___
19. Losing a game .... 1 ___ 2 ___ 3 ___ 4 ___ 5 ___
20. Being invited to a party .... 1 ___ 2 ___ 3 ___ 4 ___ 5 ___
21. The sound of a gun shot ...... 1 ___ 2 ___ 3 ___ 4 ___ 5 ___
22. Being the center of attention .... 1 ___ 2 ___ 3 ___ 4 ___ 5 ___
23. A large barking dog .... 1 ___ 2 ___ 3 ___ 4 ___ 5 ___
24. Overhearing gossip about yourself .. 1 ___ 2 ___ 3 ___ 4 ___ 5 ___
25. Not being invited to a party .... 1 ___ 2 ___ 3 ___ 4 ___ 5 ___

RELAXATION

DIFFUSING STRESS

> Learning to manage stressful situations is an important life skill. This activity helps children identify specific things they can employ to diffuse stress.

OBJECTIVES Children will:
- Review and discuss a variety of stress-reduction techniques.
- Identify new techniques that they would like to try.

MATERIALS One copy of the experience sheet "Comfort Yourself" for each child

DIRECTIONS Give each child a copy of the experience sheet.

Read through the list of suggestions with the children, focusing briefly on one technique at a time. Ask for a show of hands from children who have tried the technique. Then ask for a show of hands from children who would *like* to try it.

Direct the children who have tried the technique to write a plus (+) mark next to the item, and the children who would like to try it to put a check (✓) mark beside the item.

As you review each strategy, discuss the types of situations in which it would work best. Ask children who have tried the technique to describe how well it worked. When the children mention additional techniques, write them on the board.

Elaborate on the importance of diffusing stressful situations, and emphasize the wide range of strategies available.

DISCUSSION QUESTIONS

1. *What can happen if you do nothing and the stress keeps building?*
1. *How does physical exercise help relieve stress?*
1. *When does talking with someone work best?*
1. *Have you ever gotten rid of stress by solving a problem?*
1. *What are some unhealthy ways to relieve stress?*

COMFORT YOURSELF
EXPERIENCE SHEET

Put a + next to suggestions for coping with stress that you have *already* tried.
Put a ✓ beside suggestions you think you might *like* to try.

____ Read a book.
____ Blow soap bubbles.
____ Sculpt modeling clay.
____ Color or draw a picture.
____ Sing songs.
____ Play your favorite game.
____ Help a friend with homework.
____ Call grandma and grandpa.
____ Work on a jigsaw puzzle.
____ Go for a jog or walk.
____ Play a computer game.
____ Build something.
____ Fix yourself some hot chocolate.
____ Play with your pet.
____ Listen to happy or relaxing music.
____ Go to a park and swing really high.
____ Watch a movie.
____ Close your eyes and breathe deeply.
____ Play an instrument.
____ Talk with a parent or other trusted adult.
____ Dance to some lively music.
____ Go for a bike ride.

HELPING FRIENDS DEAL WITH STRESS

> Sometimes it is easier to identify how to help someone else rather than yourself. Through this activity, designed to consider was to help a friend dealing with a stressful situation, the children are also learning how to help themselves.

OBJECTIVES Children will:
- Name ways to recognize signs of stress in others.
- Describe specific ways of helping friends deal with stress.

MATERIALS One copy of the experience sheet "10 Ways to Help a Friend in Distress" for each child

DIRECTIONS Begin by asking the children: "Have you ever been around a friend who was stressed out?" Ask for a show of hands and comment on the number who respond (probably the majority). Then ask: "How did you know that your friend was stressed out?"

Call on volunteers to describe clues that led them to their conclusions. Try to cover such common symptoms as a flushed, worried, or tense appearance; erratic, sullen, or hyper behavior; angry outbursts; and acting distracted or withdrawn. In many cases, the friends may simply have *shared* that they were stressed out.

Ask for a show of hands from children who tried to help their stressed-out friends. Facilitate sharing and discussion about the methods they used. List ideas on the board.

Distribute the experience sheets and go over the directions. Give the children about five minutes to write down as many ideas as they can think of. Then have the children form groups of three. Tell them to share their lists in the group and then brainstorm additional ideas. Suggest that each person record all of the ideas generated by the group. Allow about 15 minutes for sharing and brainstorming.

Reconvene the class and ask one person from each group to read that group's list. Comment on specific ideas to generate discussion and jot new ideas on the board. If the following ideas are not mentioned, suggest them yourself.

- Be a good listener.
- Express sympathy; say you are sorry that your friend feels stressed.
- Offer to go for a walk or bike ride with your friend.
- Suggest a game to play together.
- Offer to help your friend think of a solution.
- Suggest an adult to talk to.
- Give your friend a shoulder massage.
- Phone or text your friend later to see how things are going.
- Offer to help your friend study (if the stress is related to tests/grades).
- Tell a trusted adult about your friend's distress. (Discuss when this is appropriate.)

DISCUSSION QUESTIONS

1. *Of the ways you have tried, which worked best?*
1. *What's a good thing to do if you have only a few minutes, or seconds, to help?*
1. *Why is it good to follow up later with a phone call, to see how your friend is doing?*
1. *When should you absolutely tell an adult? When should you avoid telling an adult?*
1. *If you felt stressed, how would you want your friends to help?*

10 WAYS TO HELP A FRIEND IN DISTRESS
EXPERIENCE SHEET

List 10 things that you can say or do to help a friend who is stressed. Describe helpful actions. Write down helpful statements word-for-word, just as if you were saying them.

1. _____
2. _____
3. _____
4. _____
5. _____
6. _____
7. _____
8. _____
9. _____
10. _____

MANY WAYS TO HANDLE STRESS

> By learning from others what they do to combat stress, children are developing a repertoire of stress management techniques.

OBJECTIVES Children will:
- Interview adults and peers to learn how they manage stress.
- Describe and compare several stress-reduction strategies.

MATERIALS One copy of the experience sheet "How Do You Handle Stress" for each child

DIRECTIONS Begin by relating the following incident to the children (or substitute a similar story from your own experience). Tell the children to listen carefully.

Four children are competing in a spelling bee (two girls and two boys) are waiting backstage for a big competition to begin. With them are a teacher and two parents. The children are competing for the state championship. The winner will not only take home a shiny engraved trophy, but he or she will also earn a trip to the national competition in Washington DC. The auditorium is filling up with people. With each passing minute, the tension builds. One girl is sitting very still with her eyes closed, breathing deeply. The other girl is getting a shoulder massage from one of the parents. One of the boys is pacing back and forth from one end of the room to the other. The second boy is listening to music on his ipod and moving to the beat. The teacher and the other parent are huddled together talking quietly.

When you have finished relating the story, ask the children to describe the different things that these seven people are doing to ease the stress of waiting. Include:

- Deep breathing
- Physical activity (pacing)

- Listening to music
- Massage
- Talking

Emphasize that every individual develops favorite ways of handling stress. Some of those ways are deliberate and helpful. Others are automatic and may be less helpful. For example, some people become chatterboxes under stress, annoying everyone around them. Others try to reduce stress by eating huge bags of potato chips. Neither of these methods is terribly helpful.

Tell the children that they are going to find out how different people handle stress and share what they learn with the class.

Distribute the experience sheets and go over the directions. Assign a completion date.

If time permits, have the children share their completed experience sheets in small groups before convening the total group. This will give everyone a chance to share at least once. In the large group, ask volunteers to describe the coping methods of one or two people they interviewed. Facilitate discussion, comparing methods and their effectiveness.

DISCUSSION QUESTIONS

1. *Which of the methods described by your interviewees seemed to work best?*
1. *What are some of the reasons that methods fail?*
1. *Why is it good to learn more than one way of coping with stress?*
1. *Which of the methods we've talked about have you tried? How well did they work?*
1. *Which new methods would you like to try?*

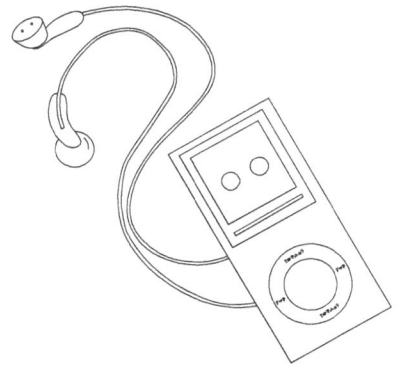

49

HOW DO YOU HANDLE STRESS?
EXPERIENCE SHEET

People handle stress in many different ways. Some of those ways work better than others. Learn how three different people cope with stress. Interview one parent, one other adult, and one friend. Write down their answers to the following questions:

PARENT

1. What do you *usually* do to cope with feelings of stress? _____
   _____

2. Does this method relieve stress? ____Yes ____ No   How quickly? _____
   _____

3. Should I try this method? ____Yes ____ No   Why or why not? _____
   _____

4. What other methods do you use? _____
   _____

ADULT

1. What do you *usually* do to cope with feelings of stress? _____
   _____

2. Does this method relieve stress? ____Yes ____ No   How quickly? _____
   _____

3. Should I try this method? ____Yes ____ No   Why or why not? _____
   _____

4. What other methods do you use? _____
   _____

FRIEND

1. What do you *usually* do to cope with feelings of stress? _____
   _____

2. Does this method relieve stress? ____Yes ____ No   How quickly? _____
   _____

3. Should I try this method? ____Yes ____ No   Why or why not? _____
   _____

4. What other methods do you use? _____
   _____

LOL FOR HEALTH

> What can be better than a good laugh to pull you out of a stressful situation? It may seem trite, but this is an important awareness to develop and children are never too young to develop strategies to engage the humor in life.

OBJECTIVES Children will:
- Laugh.
- Describe how laughing makes them feel.
- Discuss the benefits of using laughter as a stress-reduction technique.

MATERIALS None

DIRECTIONS Write the heading "Laughter" on the board and introduce the activity by stating: "Today we're going to talk about laughter, the most powerful stress buster of them all. Better yet, in addition to *talking* about laughter, we are going to laugh."

Ask for a show of hands from children who have laughed at least once that day. Acknowledge the number, whether many or few. Then, one at a time, write the following synonyms on the board, and ask, "Was it a _____?"

- Tee-hee
- Giggle
- Chuckle
- Roar
- Belly laugh
- Snicker
- Chortle
- Yuk
- Howl
- Side-splitting crack up

While counting the hands for each type of laughter, ask various children to demonstrate how each one looks and sounds. For example, say, "Show us what a 'snicker' looks like, Shelly," or "Show us how a chortle is different from a chuckle, Ruben."

Get everyone involved in mimicking the various demonstrations. Ham it up, asking the demonstrator (and the class), "Is this right?" and "Does Mark have it, or is that more of a belly laugh?"

When the demonstrations are finished and the class has quieted down, ask the children how they feel. Facilitate a discussion about the effects of laughter. Point out that laughter is not only fun, it is healthy. It reduces stress quickly and effectively while at the same time increasing:

- Relaxation
- Blood flow to the brain and body
- Alertness and productivity
- Positive feelings
- Ability to remember
- Creativity
- Ability to solve problems and resolve conflicts

Ask the children what makes them laugh. Call on volunteers to describe the things they find truly funny, such as particular TV shows, comedians, comic actors, cartoons, and funny friends and relatives. Expand the discussion to include the use of humor as a deliberate conflict-resolution strategy as well as a stress-reduction strategy.

DISCUSSION QUESTIONS

1. *When have you used humor to help resolve a conflict? How well did it work?*
1. *Have you ever defused someone's anger by saying something funny? Tell us about it.*
1. *What can you do at home to trigger laughter when you are feeling stressed?*
1. *When you feel stressed at school, what can you do to lighten up?*
1. *What does it mean when someone says, "He has a good sense of humor"?*
1. *How can you develop a good sense of humor?*

RELAXATION THREE WAYS

> The essence of stress reduction is relaxation. You can repeatedly urge mindfulness and relaxation, explaining in detail their value, but until you actually *teach* and *routinely practice* methods to accomplish these objectives — prior to tests, following breaks, as transitions from active to quiet tasks — nothing much will change. These three relaxation techniques are provided because they are easy to teach and highly effective.

OBJECTIVES Children will:
- Learn and practice three relaxation techniques.
- Understand the purpose of each technique.
- Compare the relative benefits of the three techniques.

MATERIALS Reasonable space and moveable chairs; optional soft instrumental music

DIRECTIONS Provided here are three distinct methods of achieving relaxation. Each is simple, easy to learn, and effective. The key to success is repetition. Have your children practice one or more of these exercises regularly. Make relaxation part of their routine. After the children have experienced the different relaxation methods, use the questions below to spark a discussion.

DISCUSSION QUESTIONS

1. *Which of the three relaxation exercises did you like best? Why?*
1. *Which exercise was most effective in helping you to relax?*
1. *Which exercise are you most apt to use on your own?*
1. *During the meditation, how difficult was it to concentrate on counting?*
1. *During the muscle relaxation exercise, where did you feel the most tension?*
1. *During what part of your day are you usually very relaxed? When are you usually very tense?*
1. *Which of these techniques could you use to relax during the tense part of your day?*

Deep Breathing

The simplest, most direct route to relaxation is that of deep breathing. Explain to the children that when they are tense, nervous, angry, or excited, their breathing becomes more rapid. Deliberately slowing and controlling the depth and rate of their breathing can help them to calm down and feel more relaxed.

Read the directions slowly, progressing from chest to abdominal (belly) breathing and then combining the movements in one slow, continuous four-count exercise.

Chest-breathing

1. Sit in a comfortable position and close your eyes.
2. Inhale and exhale deeply through your nose three times.
3. Place your left hand on your stomach, just below your ribs. Place your right hand on your chest.
4. Breathe normally and notice where your breath is coming from.
5. Now take a long, slow, deep breath into your chest. Your right hand will rise while your left hand remains fairly still.
6. Pause briefly, keeping your chest full, then exhale slowly through your nose.
7. Repeat this "chest breathing" three times.
8. Breathe in, hold, release... breathe in, hold, release... breathe in, hold, release.
9. Breathe normally.

Belly-breathing

1. Now, take a long, slow deep breath into your stomach. Your left hand will rise, while your right hand remains fairly still.
2. Pause briefly, feeling your stomach muscles push up, then exhale slowly through your nose.
3. Repeat this "belly breathing" three times.
4. Breathe in, hold, release... breathe in, hold, release... breathe in, hold, release.
5. Breathe normally.

Combined chest-belly breathing

1. Count one: breathe into your belly (left hand rises)
2. Count two: breathe into your chest (right hand rises)
3. Count three: Exhale from your belly (left hand lowers)
4. Count four: Exhale from your chest (right hand lowers)
5. Pause.
6. Repeat: one... two... three... four...
7. Continue for 2-3 minutes.

5-Minute Meditation

Explain to the children that the purpose of meditation is to relax the body and quiet the mind. Point out that our bodies are usually active and moving. Even while sitting, we tend to shift, turn, and twitch. Similarly, our minds never stop producing thoughts, not even during sleep. By sitting quietly for a few minutes while breathing naturally and focusing all of our attention on a particular sound, we can calm both mind and body.

In this exercise the children will focus on the sound of their own voice counting from one to four. Have the children move their chairs to create maximum distance from one another. If possible, they should face blank walls, or at least face away from other children. A circle, with everyone turned to face out, works well. Tell the children to count very quietly, just above a whisper.

Slowly read these directions:

1. Sit straight in your chair. Fold your hands in your lap or rest them on your thighs.
1. Look down slightly with your eyes, keeping your head straight.
1. Sit quietly and try not to move. Breathe naturally.

Pause briefly, then continue…

1. Focus your attention on your breathing.
1. Silently count "one" as you inhale. Count "two" as you exhale. Count "three" as you inhale. Count "four" as you exhale.
1. Continue breathing in and out with each count up to ten.
1. Start over, breathing and counting up to ten.
1. Concentrate on the sound of your own voice counting. If other thoughts enter your mind, that's okay. Just let them pass and go back to focusing on your voice.
1. Continue for 5 minutes.

Progressive Muscle Relaxation

One of the best ways to differentiate a tense muscle from a relaxed one, thereby guaranteeing relaxation, is to first exaggerate the tension. Progressive muscle relaxation helps children feel the difference by tensing and relaxing one muscle group at a time, from toe to head. As you read the directions, exaggerate your inflexion to convey the alternate sensations of tension and relaxation. Play the role of coach.

1. Sit or lie in a comfortable position with your eyes closed. Breathe naturally.
1. Think about each set of muscles as I tell you to tense and hold for 5 seconds. Try to move only the muscles I tell you to move, keeping the rest of your body still. Notice how it feels. Then notice the difference when I tell you to relax those muscles.
1. Tense your toes by flexing them as though you were standing on tiptoe. Hold. Relax.
1. Flex your ankles and move them around in circles. Flex again. Hold. Relax.
1. Tense and stretch your calf muscles by pushing hard with your heels. Hold. Relax.
1. Tense the large muscles in your thighs. Hold. Relax.
1. Tense your hip and buttocks muscles. Feel your hips lift. Hold. Relax.
1. Tense your abdominal muscles. Feel them tighten. Hold. Relax.
1. Tense your stomach muscles. Suck them in as tightly as you can. Hold. Relax.
1. Make tight fists with your fingers. Tighter. Hold. Relax.
1. Flex your wrists. Make circles with your wrists. Flex again. Hold. Relax.
1. Tense the muscles in your arms. Make your arms as stiff as boards. Hold. Relax.
1. Tense your shoulder muscles. Hunch your shoulders up to your ears. Hold. Relax.
1. Tense your neck by touching your chin to your collarbone. Hold. Relax.
1. Turn your neck as far as it will go to the right. Hold. Relax.
1. Turn your neck as far as it will go to the left. Hold. Relax.
1. Scrunch all the muscles of your face as tightly as you can. Hold. Relax.
1. Now tense your whole body, starting with your toes all the way up to your face. Hold. Relax.

CALMING NOTES

> Music is a great way to calm the body and mind. This activity allows the children to directly and consciously experience the benefit.

OBJECTIVES Children will:
- ♥ Relax to quiet music.
- ♥ Describe how music can be used to reduce stress.

MATERIALS Relaxing instrumental music

DIRECTIONS Talk with the children about using music to promote relaxation and stress reduction. Acknowledge that while everyone has particular tastes in music, when the goal is to relax, not just any music will do. Fast, rhythmic music energizes us and makes us want to move. Lyrics inspire us to sing along. So when we want to relax our minds and bodies, it's better to choose quiet music with a slow beat and no vocals.

Play excerpts from two or three selections of relaxing music. Suggest that the children close their eyes while they listen. Then ask the children what they think of the music. Tell them a little about the composer and/or performer.

Next, play a longer selection while you lead the children in a simple guided relaxation. Pause for a few moments between sentences as you softly repeat these directions:

Settle back in a comfortable position and close your eyes. Mentally scan your body. Notice which muscles are tense and which are relaxed, and where you feel pain. Be aware of your mood. Now, focus all of your attention on the music. When unrelated thoughts cross your mind, just let them pass. Allow the music to relax the parts of your body that feel tense. Complete relaxation is your goal. Say to yourself, "Relax... relax... relax..."

When the music ends, tell the children to remain where they are, with their eyes closed. After a full minute, state:

Without opening your eyes, scan your body again. Be aware of how it feels. Does your body feel different than it did before you started? Is there any difference in your mood?

Have the children open their eyes. Facilitate a brief discussion about the experience.

DISCUSSION QUESTIONS

1. *What differences do you notice in your body since doing the exercise?*
1. *How has your mood changed?*
1. *How difficult was it to concentrate on the music?*
1. *Do you relax to music at home? What kind of music?*
1. *What have you learned today about reducing stress?*

SUCCESS STRATEGIES

WHO CAN HELP?

It's always valuable to have someone to talk with in times of stress and anxiety. This activity prompts children to identify who they can go to with problems, thereby, making it more likely they actually will when they are in need.

OBJECTIVES The Children will:

- Identify sources of help and support for stressful times.
- Describe situations where help or adult intervention may be needed.

MATERIALS One copy of the experience sheet "The Road to Help" for each child

DIRECTIONS Initiate a discussion about stressful situations that demand help or intervention from others, particularly adults. Describe a few examples and ask the children to think of others, such as:

- Being bullied or harassed
- Falling behind in school
- Grieving the loss of a family member or close friend
- Abuse of any kind from anyone

Emphasize that the children do not have to deal with stressful situations and difficult problems alone. There are many people both able and willing to assist them when they need help.

Distribute the experience sheets and go over the directions. Give the children a few minutes to complete the sheet. Then discuss the results as a group.

DISCUSSION QUESTIONS

1. *Which of the remaining words describe people that you could go to for help?*
1. *Why are some problems too big to handle alone?*
1. *What could happen if you didn't get help?*
1. *What can you do if you are fearful or shy about asking for help?*
1. *When have you asked for help and been glad you did?*

THE ROAD TO HELP
EXPERIENCE SHEET

When you are upset or have a problem, share your feelings with someone you trust. It helps!

Follow these directions:

1. Draw a line through all the words that name an animal.
2. Draw a line through all the words that name a place.
3. Draw a line through all the words that name a number.
4. Draw a line through all the words that name a thing.
5. Draw a line through all the words that name a toy.
6. Look at what's left. Circle the words that name someone you could ask for help.

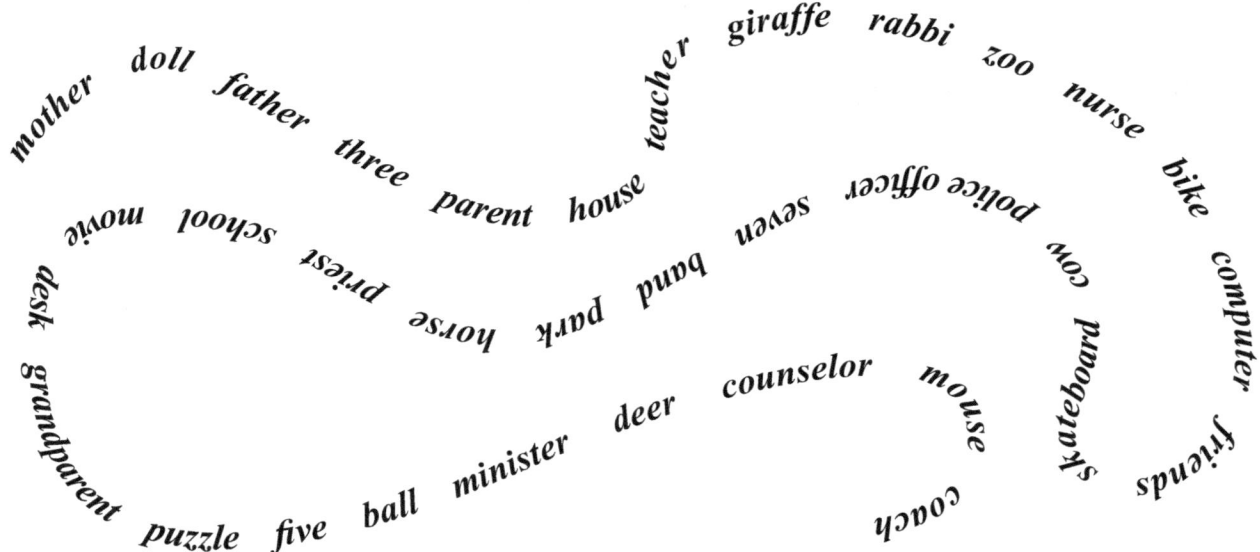

Your problems may seem unique, but they are not. Most people have dealt with similar problems. When you reach out for help, you can learn from the experience and ideas of others. Don't forget, adults were your age once.

Name three people who you can ask for help when you have a problem.

1. _____
2. _____
3. _____

Are you willing to ask these people for help?____ Yes ____ No

Copyright © Innerchoice Publishing

WHAT'S YOUR SELF-TALK

> Many people have a tendency to put themselves down when they have fallen short in something. A very important life skill is knowing how to reframe one's self talk to be positive, supportive and self encouraging rather than bringing oneself down. This activity teaches children how to do so.

OBJECTIVES Children will:

- ❤ Define the term *self-talk*.
- ❤ Give examples of negative and positive self-talk.
- ❤ Discuss methods for improving their own self-talk.

MATERIALS One copy of the experience sheet "What Do You Say When You Talk To Yourself" for each child

DIRECTIONS Ask if anyone can explain the meaning of the term "self-talk." Call on volunteers, and help the children reason that self-talk is *talk we direct at ourselves*. Explain:

Self-talk consists of the things you say <u>about</u> yourself <u>to</u> yourself. It can also refer to judgments you make about yourself when talking to someone else. For example, telling yourself or someone else that you are "lousy at math" is what we call negative self-talk. When you say things about yourself that are negative, you are programming your brain to make you behave in those negative ways. When you say positive things about yourself, you are directing your brain to make you behave in positive ways.

Write the headings "Positive Self-talk" and "Negative Self-talk" on the board. Ask the children to help you brainstorm a list of statements under each heading. Suggest that they recall statements they and their friends commonly make to themselves. List items such as:

NEGATIVE	POSITIVE
I'm basically lazy.	I'm good at that.
I can't do puzzles.	I always do well in science.
I hate school.	They like me because I'm funny.
Nobody likes me.	I did the best drawing.

Distribute the experience sheet. Tell the children that you want them to pay attention to their self-talk for the next few days and record on the experience sheet how many times they catch themselves saying negative as well as positive things about themselves. Explain that the experience sheet also contains tips to help them improve their self-talk. Discuss the tips and suggest specific ways to put them to use. Remind the children that they will benefit from making a deliberate effort to improve their self-talk.

DISCUSSION QUESTIONS

1. *What feelings usually accompany negative thoughts or statements about yourself?*
1. *What feelings accompany positive thoughts or statements about yourself?*
1. *How could saying "I'm lousy at spelling" possibly help you in spelling?*
1. *If it doesn't help to say such things, why do we say them?*
1. *How can you help a friend improve his/her self-talk? How can your friend help you?*

WHAT DO YOU SAY WHEN YOU TALK TO YOURSELF?

EXPERIENCE SHEET

For the next three days pay close attention to your self-talk. Keep track of how often you say negative and positive things to yourself. Put a check (✔) in the negative block each time you say something negative to yourself. Each time you say something positive about yourself, put a (✔) in the positive block.

NEGATIVE	POSITIVE

Pay attention to the self-talk you hear others say. Check (✔) either the negative or positive blocks below when you hear others using either negative or positive self-talk.

NEGATIVE	POSITIVE

Think of negative self-talk as a bad habit. Replace it with something better. Create two positive self-talk statements you can say about yourself.

1. _____

2. _____

Try to use positive self-talk daily.

Tell others how to use positive self-talk.

PROBLEM-SOLVING GUIDELINES

Personal problems are a major cause of stress. Helping children understand that there are specific actions they can take to help solve problems can give them a feeling of control and help alleviate the stress caused by feeling overwhelmed and out of control. This activity provides chidren with age-appropriate steps they can take to solve problems.

OBJECTIVES The children will:

- understand and describe how decisions are influenced.
- develop and practice a process for effective problem solveing.

MATERIALS One copy of the experience sheet, "Steps for Solving a Problem" for each child

DIRECTIONS Ask the children to raise their hands if they have ever had to deal with a problem. Raise your hand as well and acknowledge that all people experience problems at times. Explain that problems can seem big or little, and people usually feel uncomfortable or even stressed out until they deal with the problem in a constructive way. Inform the children that the important thing to know is that there are very specific steps that can be taken to help anyone solve a problem.

Distribute the experience sheet, and go over the directions. Provide time for the children to complete their sheets and then review which "steps" they crossed off and which they checked as appropriate to solving problems. As you discuss each step, talk about why certain steps are not wise and why it's a good idea to know and use the other steps.

In reviewing the steps the children chose for solving problems be sure to ask the following questions about each to facilitate discussion and encourage reflection on each problem-solving step.

DISCUSSION QUESTIONS

Identify the problem –

   1. Why is it important to know exactly what the problem is?

Make sure it's your problem and not someone else's –

   1. Why does it matter if it's your problem or someone else's?
   2. What can happen when a person gets all worked up about a problem that isn't their own?

Ask for help when necessary –

   1. When is it wise to ask for help?
   2. When should people not be left to solve their own problems?
   3. If what you want is information or advice, and instead the person tries to solve the problem for you, what can you do?

Collect information that can help you solve the problem –

   1. Where can you go to gather information?
   2. Who can you ask for advice when you have a problem?

Think of alternative solutions and consider the consequences of each alternative –

   1. What is the advantage of thinking of lots of alternatives?
   2. How could collecting information expand your alternatives?
   3. Why is it important to imagine what will happen as a result of trying each alternative?
   4. Why not just do the first thing that comes to mind?

Make a decision –

   1. Why stick to a decision
   2. What can you do if the solution doesn't work or more problems come up?
   3. How can you evalutate your deicision?

STEPS FOR SOLVING A PROBLEM
EXPERIENCE SHEET

What is a problem? A problem can be as simple as a question you have to answer, or it can be a big thing in your life that is causing you worry, anger, frustration, or some other kind of distress. In order to answer the question or get rid of the stress you must "solve" the problem.

Solving problems often involves several steps. Below is a list of steps both helpful and unhelpful for solving problems. Read through the list and cross out any steps that you think wouldn't be helpful in solving a problem. Put a check (✔) in front of each step that you think would be helpful.

___ Ignore the problem.

___ Identify the problem—Think the problem through and be sure you know exactly what the problem is.

___ Have a bad attitude about the problem.

___ Make sure it's your problem and not someone else's.

___ Don't do anything about the problem because you're afraid of making a mistake.

___ Ask for help when necessary.

___ Hope you'll be lucky and the problem will go away.

___ Collect information that can help you solve the problem.

___ Think of alternative solutions and consider the consequences of each one.

___ Ask someone to solve your problem for you.

___ Make a decision and follow through on it—Give it time, but if it doesn't work, try another alternative.

Don't get discouraged—

Remember, on the way to success you'll make mistakes.

MANAGING TIME

One of the primary causes of stress is poor time management which often leaves people rushing to complete some tasks while forgetting to do others or not allowing enough time to complete a task. Children need to start early in developing an understanding of what they can do to effectively manage time.

OBJECTIVES   Children will:
- Review and discuss time-management skills and techniques.
- Share additional time-management strategies they have tried.

MATERIALS   One copy of the experience sheet "Managing Your Time" for each child

DIRECTIONS   Distribute the experience sheets. Read through the time management tips with the children. Elaborate with examples from your own experience, or the experience of other children you've worked with. Facilitate discussion.

Urge the children to enlist the help of their parents in setting up some of the recommended conditions. Suggest they keep the experience sheets. Occasionally check to see how many have followed the advice provided.

DISCUSSION QUESTIONS

1. Where do you usually study?
2. How well is your study area organized?
3. What tools or supplies do you almost always need for studying?
4. Why do people keep calendars?
5. What would happen if no one wrote down things like medical appointments?
6. Which of the tips on the list do you already use? Which are the most helpful?
7. What are your best study hours?
8. Which of the tips do you think will help you the most?
9. What other ideas do you have for managing time wisely?

MANAGING YOUR TIME
EXPERIENCE SHEET

1. Get ORGANIZED.
   Keep your room and study area neat and organized. Have things like paper, pencils, eraser, and paper clips nearby. If you use a computer, label files clearly and save them to a "work" folder.

2. Write a daily TO-DO LIST.
   Write down the things you plan to do each day. Cross them off the list when they are done.

3. Learn good STUDY SKILLS.
   Write down assignments. Do the hardest things first. As you read, write down questions to ask the teacher. Outline chapters, or draw diagrams to help you remember what you're learning.

4. Get enough SLEEP.
   To stay alert and healthy, you need eight or nine hours every night. Your brain is very busy while you sleep. Give it plenty of time to do its work.

5. Don't OVERDO.
   Leave a little time every day for yourself. Time to relax, be with friends, play with your pet, or just do nothing. When you try to do too much, the quality of your work may suffer. Your health may suffer, too.

6. Learn to say NO.
   You don't have to do everything that your friends do. If you are too busy to join them, just say so. Take charge of your time and your choices.

Copyright © Innerchoice Publishing

HIGH-STAKES TESTING

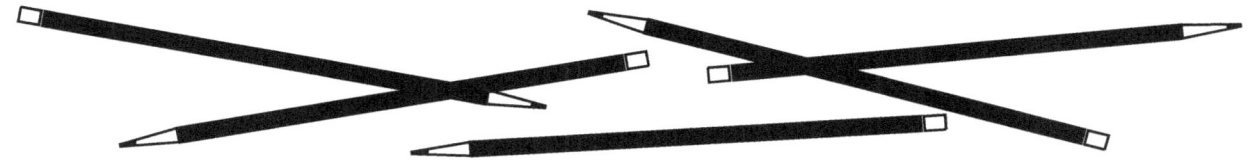

STRATEGIES FOR HANDLING TEST ANXIETY

With so much riding on test scores today it's only natural that many children respond to testing with high levels of anxiety. These next two activities help children learn and practice stress reduction strategies which can help them perform better on tests.

OBJECTIVES Children will:

- Describe the physical and psychological effects of test anxiety.
- Compare imagined consequences of failure with realistic consequences.
- Identify stress-reduction techniques that can be used to reduce test anxiety.

MATERIALS One copy of the experience sheet "Easing Test Anxiety" for each child

DIRECTIONS Begin by discussing the concept of test anxiety. Ask the children how much they worry about upcoming tests, the extent to which their lives are disrupted by test anxiety, and how they usually handle it.

At some point in the discussion, ask: "What is the absolute worst thing that could happen if you didn't do well on a test?" Encourage the children to describe the most extreme consequences they can think of. Then ask, "Okay, now that we've imagined the very worst, what do you think would *really* happen?"

Contrast the differences between the children' imaginings and their reality. Point out that the emotions experienced during extreme test anxiety are

usually not reality-based. They are better suited to a natural disaster than they are to a test. That is why it's so important to learn and practice stress-reduction skills.

Distribute the experience sheets and go over the directions. Give the children a few minutes to complete the sheets. Then call on volunteers to read items from their lists. Record ideas for reducing test anxiety on the board and discuss ways to implement them prior to and during a test.

DISCUSSION QUESTIONS

1. *What can you do if you know an answer, but your mind goes blank?*
1. *Why is it important to get lots of sleep the night before a test?*
1. *Why is cramming for a test a bad idea?*
1. *What messages can you give yourself (self talk) to help reduce test anxiety?*
1. *What breathing exercises can you use? When should you use them?*

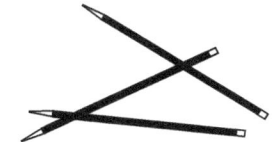

EASING TEST ANXIETY
EXPERIENCE SHEET

Tests can be stressful. Even if you study hard, you can still mess up. Lots of worrying about the test only makes the situation worse. But stress can be managed. You have learned several ways to reduce stress and feel more relaxed. Next time you are anxious about a test, try some of those strategies.

DIRECTIONS

In the left-hand column, list ways in which test anxiety affects you (upset stomach, headache, jitters, forgetfulness, etc.). In the right-hand column, list things that you can do reduce the stress.

HOW TEST ANXIETY AFFECTS ME   WHAT I CAN DO TO LOWER THE ANXIETY

1. _____   • _____
2. _____   • _____
3. _____   • _____
4. _____   • _____
5. _____   • _____
6. _____   • _____
7. _____   • _____
8. _____   • _____
9. _____   • _____
10. _____   • _____

Copyright © Innerchoice Publishing

HELPING KIDS WITH TEST ANXIETY

OBJECTIVES Children will:
- Describe how test taking affects them emotionally.
- Discuss the importance of reducing the stress of test taking.
- Learn stress-reduction strategies to use in testing situations.

MATERIALS One copy of the experience sheet "Tips For Managing Test Anxiety" for each child

DIRECTIONS Explain to the children that test anxiety is normal and usually not a problem. It's a type of *performance* fear—like feeling nervous before making a speech or playing in a music recital. It can help focus your mind and improve performance.

Extreme anxiety, on the other hand, can be debilitating. Chemicals released by the brain can block memory and result in a lower score. That's why it's important to learn ways to control stress levels, particularly at test time.

Ask the children to recall a recent test situation and describe how they felt just before the test. Write their contributions on the board. Include feelings such as:

- Scared
- Confident
- Relaxed
- Annoyed
- Jittery
- Paralyzed

Distribute the experience sheets and go over the stress-reduction strategies with the children. Elaborate on each one and generate additional suggestions from the group. Suggest that the children keep the sheets handy as a reminder of things they can do to lessen test stress.

DISCUSSION QUESTIONS

1. *Why do teachers and schools give so many tests?*
1. *What's the best way to make sure you do well on tests?*
1. *What should you do if you don't understand a test question?*
1. *Is it okay to guess if you don't know the answer? Why or why not?*
1. *Which methods of reducing test stress do you already use?*
1. *What new method do you plan to try?*

TIPS FOR MANAGING TEST ANXIETY
EXPERIENCE SHEET

**Having a test? Don't let stress ruin your day – or your score.
Take these steps to lower stress.**

1. **Prepare.** Read. Do your homework. Ask questions. Enjoy learning. If you do these things, your test scores will be fine.

2. **Get lots of sleep.** Your brain and body need rest. Sleep at least eight hours the night before a test.

3. **Eat healthy food.** Good food makes for a good performance. Skip the sugary stuff. Eat nuts and fruits instead, and don't forget to eat breakfast.

4. **Think positive.** Tell yourself that you are going to do exceptionally well on the test. Believe it! Avoid negative, discouraging thoughts. Focus your thoughts on being ready, relaxed, and confident.

5. **Picture success.** Imagine yourself calmly taking the test and remembering everything you need to know. Have this daydream often.

6. **Ask for help.** If you still get very nervous before tests, talk it over with your teacher or counselor. They can help.

7. **Take a deep breath.** Deep breathing really helps you body to relax. Whenever you are feeling tense or anxious, either before or during a test, stop and take several deep breaths. Breathe in through your nose, hold the breath, and then slowly breathe out through your mouth. Make sure you can feel your breathing in your stomach. That's how you know it's deep breathing. Practice this often, and use it during stressful moments.

   Which method of stress reduction have you used? _____

   _____

   What new method will you try? _____

   _____

TEST PREP RELAXATION TECHNIQUE

This activity allows children to practice a relaxation and breathing experience that can be used prior to a test or anytime they are feeling anxious and stressed to calm themselves down.

OBJECTIVES Children will:

- Practice deep breathing and relaxation techniques.
- Visualize themselves performing well on a test.
- Describe ways of maintaining confidence during actual tests.

MATERIALS None

DIRECTIONS Tell the children that you are going to lead them in a short guided visualization that will help them perform well on tests. (If possible, time this activity to precede an actual achievement test, or other significant test.)

Sit in a comfortable position with your hands in your lap and your eyes closed. Take several deep breaths. With each in-breath, feel your body grow warm and calm. With each out-breath, feel your muscles relax.

Gradually let go of any tension. Feel your arms and shoulders relax. Feel your neck and back relax. Let the warmth and relaxation spread to your stomach and hips. Feel it extend to your legs and feet. Continue to focus on your breathing as your entire body relaxes.

Now picture yourself in class. It is test day. You know that it is test day and yet you are completely relaxed. You are confident. You know that you will do your best work. Picture your teacher passing out the test. See the test booklet (paper) in front of you on your desk. Your hands are steady and your mind is calm. You are completely confident and relaxed.

Hear the teacher telling you to start. Picture yourself calmly opening the test booklet and reading the directions. They are clear and you understand them. You feel completely relaxed and ready to begin.

Imagine yourself answering the questions, one at a time. You are alert and relaxed. Your thinking is clear. You can remember what you have learned. Your brain supplies the answers.

As you work through the test, see yourself pausing occasionally to stretch and take a few deep breaths. When you go back to the test, feel yourself refreshed and eager to continue.

Now, think to yourself, "On test day I am relaxed and alert, calm and confident."

When you are ready, open your eyes and come back to the present.

Give the children a few moments to come back to reality. Then facilitate a follow-up discussion.

DISCUSSION QUESTIONS

1. *Why is it important to stay relaxed during tests?*
1. *What can you do if you feel yourself getting worried or tense during a test?*
1. *Why do teachers give tests? Why do schools give achievement tests?*
1. *Why do most people feel nervous before a test?*
1. *How does it help to picture yourself doing well on a test?*

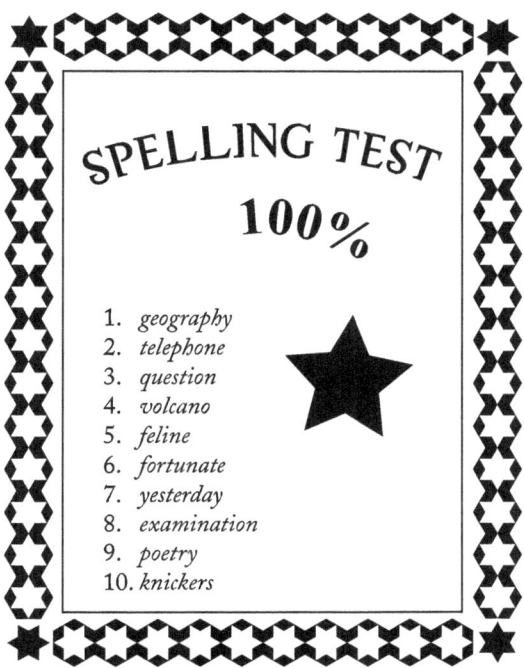

ANGER AND WORRY

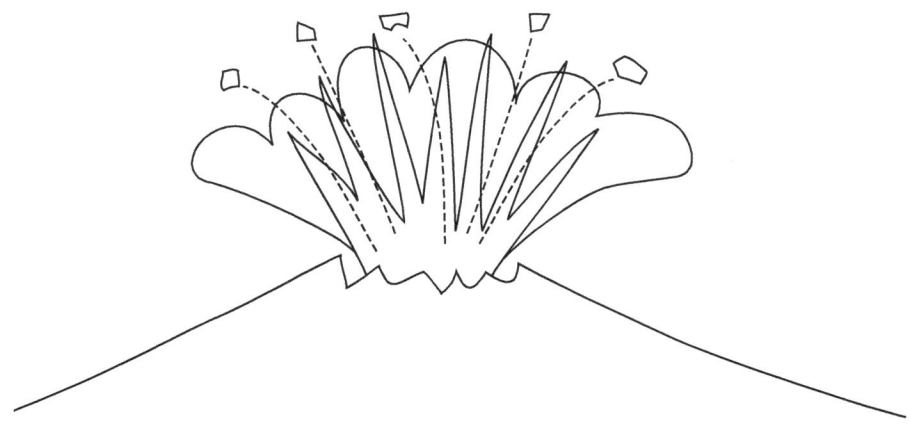

HOW ANGER MAKES ME FEEL

Anger can be a major cause of stress and also a reaction to a stressful situation. A first step to managing anger is to recognize the physical and emotional "feelings" of anger one experiences. This activity helps children identify and acknowledge their experience of anger.

OBJECTIVES Children will:
- Identify feelings and sensations associated with anger.
- Graphically describe how anger makes them feel.
- Discuss the importance of controlling anger.

MATERIALS One copy of the experience sheet "How Anger Feels" for each child

DIRECTIONS Begin by facilitating a discussion about the feelings and sensations generated by anger. For example, ask:

- How does your body feel when you are angry?
- What happens to your energy level when you are angry?
- How well are you able to study?
- What affect does being angry have on sleep?

Distribute the experience sheets. Review the list of responses on the first page. Ask for a show of hands from children who have experienced each one as a result of being angry. Invite volunteers to elaborate, describe specific situations (no names), and suggest other feelings and sensations generated by anger.

Go over the directions for the second page of the experience sheets, and give the children a few minutes to complete it. Conduct a debriefing session. Ask volunteers to share their drawings and describe the feelings and sensations represented. Discuss what the children have observed about anger and what it does to their bodies and minds. Conclude by reminding children that they have the power to control anger.

DISCUSSION QUESTIONS

1. *What kinds of things make you angry?*
1. *What do you usually do when you are angry?*
1. *What helps you get over being angry?*
1. *How does it feel to be around someone who is very angry?*
1. *Why should people avoid making decisions when they are angry?*

HOW ANGER FEELS
EXPERIENCE SHEET

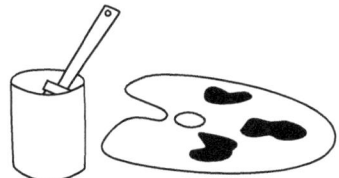

Think about times you have been angry. Put a (✓) mark in front of any item that describes you when you are angry.

___ My stomach churns.
___ My head hurts.
___ I clench my teeth.
___ My face turns hot and red.
___ My heart races.
___ My body trembles.
___ My brain gets jumbled and I can't think clearly.
___ I feel like screaming.
___ I feel like crying.
___ My facial features scowl, frown, or grimace.
___ I want to hit something with my fists.

List other feelings here:

- _____
- _____
- _____

Copyright © Innerchoice Publishing

DIRECTIONS

Using the outline below, draw a picture of yourself when you are angry. Draw your angry features. Use colors and symbols to show how your body feels when you are angry.

Anger is normal. Everyone feels angry sometimes. But anger is a powerful emotion. It can make you feel terrible. And it can make you say and do things that you later regret.

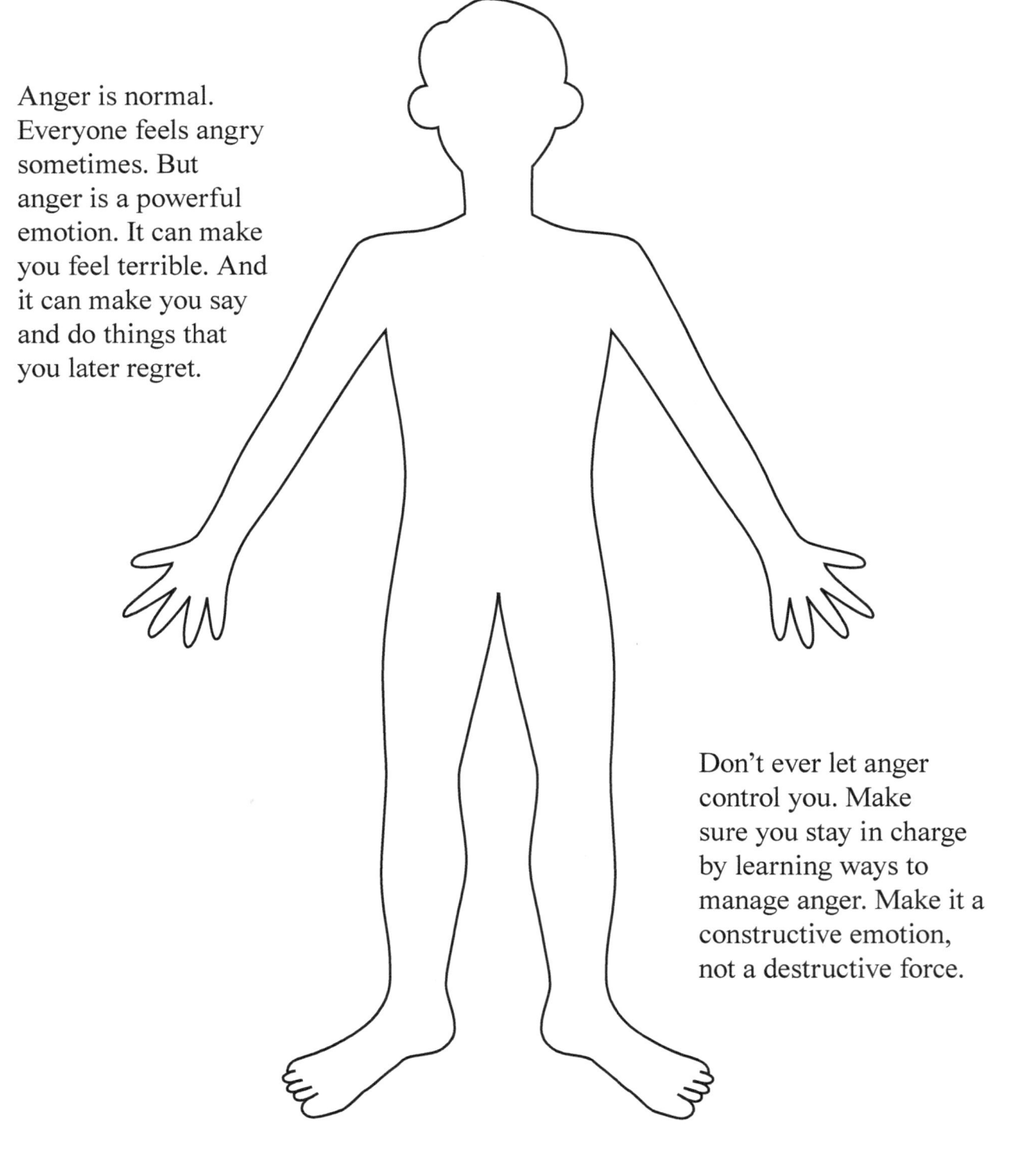

Don't ever let anger control you. Make sure you stay in charge by learning ways to manage anger. Make it a constructive emotion, not a destructive force.

CAUSES OF ANGER

> When children are able to identify situations that make them angry, can recognize the feelings of anger coming on, and have strategies for calming down, they are far more likely to handle upsetting events and people in an appropriate fashion. This activity, and the next, are designed to enlighten children in these areas.

OBJECTIVES Children will:
- ❤ Identify people, conditions, and situations that tend to make them angry.
- ❤ Describe constructive ways to manage their anger.

MATERIALS One copy of the experience sheet "What Sets Me Off" for each child

DIRECTIONS Engage the children in a discussion about anger. Acknowledge that it is an uncomfortable emotion that can sometimes be difficult to control. However, emphasize that it is normal to feel angry at times, and that anger can play a useful role in day-to-day life. Make these additional points:

- Anger is a normal human emotion. It is neither bad nor good.
- Sometimes anger serves a protective function.
- Volatile expressions of anger, if they happen often, can have negative health consequences.
- There are healthy and appropriate ways to manage anger.
- It is how we react to a situation, not the situation itself, that causes anger and other emotions.

Distribute the experience sheets and go over the directions. Give the children a few minutes to list situations and conditions that make them angry and ways to manage the anger. When they have finished, ask volunteers to read some of their items to the group. Elaborate on each example and use it to generate further discussion. Focus less on the situations (and their justification) and more on anger-management strategies.

DISCUSSION QUESTIONS

1. *Why is it important to control anger?*
1. *What are the most common causes of anger in our group?*
1. *What ideas for controlling anger work best for you?*
1. *What new ideas for controlling anger would you like to try?*
1. *What can you do if nothing you try helps to lessen your anger?*

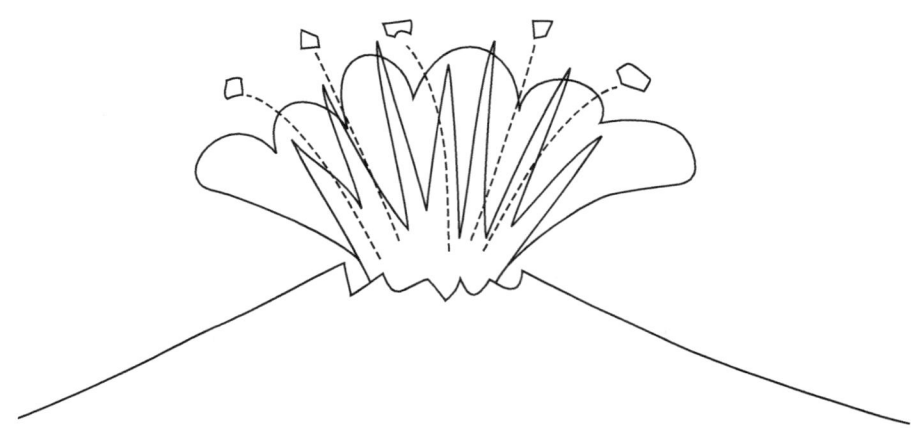

WHAT SETS ME OFF
EXPERIENCE SHEET

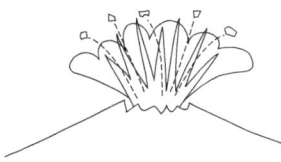
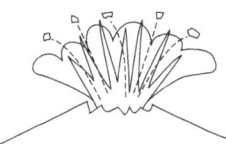

Do certain things almost always make you angry? Do you react angrily to the same situations—or the same people—over and over? Maybe you get angry when you don't get your way. Or when your brother or sister uses your things without asking.

In the left column, list things that usually make you angry. In the right column, list things you can do to deal with your angry feelings.

What Makes Me Angry	What I Can Do
1.	
2.	
3.	
4.	
5.	
6.	
7.	
8.	
9.	
10.	

TAMING TEMPERS

OBJECTIVES Children will:
- Brainstorm ways of defusing negative energy before it erupts in anger.
- Commit to testing specific anger-management strategies.

MATERIALS One copy of the experience sheet "Tips for Taming Your Temper" for each child

DIRECTIONS Ask the children to think of ways they can appropriately express the energy that builds up inside as a result of anger. Write their suggestions on the board and discuss.

Divide the class into groups of three or four. Have the groups brainstorm additional acceptable ways of dealing with anger. Ask each group to share two or three ideas with the class.

Remind the children that if they know what makes them angry, they can learn to recognize the onset of angry feelings and can do something to calm down or cool down.

Distribute the experience sheets and read through the temper-taming tips together. Give the children a few minutes to complete the sheet by listing five ideas they are willing to try the next few times they feel themselves getting angry.

DISCUSSION QUESTIONS

1. *Why is it important to learn techniques for managing anger?*
1. *What happens when people are unable to control their anger?*
1. *What techniques for reducing anger have worked for you?*
1. *Why is physical exercise so effective at reducing anger?*
1. *What happens if you let anger build up inside over hours or days?*

TIPS FOR TAMING YOUR TEMPER
EXPERIENCE SHEET

- Ride a bike
- Go for a jog
- Fast dance to loud music
- Skateboard
- Scream into a pillow
- Hit a stuffed toy
- Jump rope
- Swim
- Skate
- Punch a pillow or punching bag
- Cry
- Write a letter and tear it up
- Talk it over with a good listener
- Talk to someone you trust
- Use conflict management strategies
- Count to 10 or higher
- Talk to yourself in a positive way
- Tense and relax your muscles
- Squeeze a ball
- Read a book
- Listen to music
- Run in place for three minutes
- Take 10 deep breaths
- Write your feelings in a journal
- Take a one-minute daydream vacation to your favorite place
- Play with a pet
- Draw or paint a picture
- Play a sport
- Play a musical instrument
- Take a hot shower or bath

List five ideas that you can use to tame your temper when you are angry. Choose from the above list, or write down ideas of your own.

1. _____
2. _____
3. _____
4. _____
5. _____

ROLE-PLAYING THE OTHER POINT OF VIEW

Being able to see the point of view of another person is a significant life skill, and one that can often help manage conflict and, thus, lead to less stress.

OBJECTIVES Children will:
- Role-play a conflict situation, playing both parts.
- Communicate the point of view of a person with whom they disagree or are angry.
- Explain how understanding the opposition's point of view can help relieve anger and resolve conflict.

MATERIALS This activity requires two moveable chairs for each participating child. After you read the directions, decide whether you want all of the children to participate at once, a few at a time, or one at a time. If you are working with mature children, you may prefer to work with one child at a time, with the other children observing and participating in a debriefing session following each imagined confrontation.

DIRECTIONS Tell the children that they are going to participate in an exercise that will help them to understand the point of view of someone with whom they are angry or have a disagreement. Explain that most people, when angry, see only one point of view—their own. But with a little imagination, it's possible to understand other points of view, which can go a long way toward resolving differences.

To begin ask the children to take a few minutes to think of a time when they were angry or had a disagreement with someone. Ask them to recall a situation that they would be willing to share. Tell them they are not to use any names but just recall the situation and the feelings involved.

Next, place pairs of chairs facing each other. Ask the children who would like to volunteer for the role play. Give the following directions to participating children:

1. Sit in one chair and face the other (empty) chair.
2. Imagine the person you are angry with seated opposite you, in the empty chair.
3. Tell the person in the empty chair the things he or she has done that upset you. Use I-messages or any other form of communication that effectively expresses your feelings.
4. After you have expressed yourself, switch chairs and imagine that you are the person with whom you are angry. For example, if you are angry at a friend, become the friend and speak from his or her point of view in response to what you just said.
5. Switch chairs and become yourself again. Respond from your own point of view.

Circulate and coach the children as they continue their individual confrontations, playing both roles and switching chairs as they represent alternate, or opposing, points of view.

Focus a follow-up discussion on the importance of trying to understand the views of others, particularly in angry and stressful situations.

DISCUSSION QUESTIONS

1. *Why is it important to understand the point of view of someone with whom you are angry or disagree?*
1. *What's the difference between understanding the other person's viewpoint and "giving in" to the other person?*
1. *What role does listening play in understanding the views of others?*
1. *What did you learn from playing the role of your "opponent" in this exercise?*
1. *What did your "opponent" learn about you?*
1. *What would happen if you had this conversation in real life? Would it help settle the problem?*

WORRIES VS. SOLUTIONS: A TEAM COMPETITION

> Just as with anger, worry is a significant contributor to stress. By helping children recognize strategies for overcoming worry, we go a long way in helping develop stress management skills.

OBJECTIVES Children will:
- ♥ Identify worries commonly experienced by children.
- ♥ Suggest solutions to common worries.

MATERIALS None

DIRECTIONS Begin by having the children brainstorm things that kids their age frequently worry about. Write the worries on the board. Encourage the children to name things related to friends, social standing, school, grades, parents, siblings, physical appearance, health, schedules, athletics, chores, organizations, and activities.

Spend a few minutes talking about the amount of time spent worrying about things that:

1. Could be resolved by putting the same energy into developing solutions, or
2. Never actually happen.

Divide the class evenly into two teams. Designate one the "Worrywarts" and the other the "Resolvers." Have the members of the two teams gather on opposite sides of the room. Ask one Worrywart and one Resolver to come to the center (or front) of the room and face each other.

Direct the Worrywart to choose one worry from the list on the board and

start worrying about it—aloud. Encourage the Worrywart to choose a worry that he or she can relate to, and then to dramatize it fully, stating all the reasons why it is such a big concern.

Direct the Resolver to offer suggestions about how to avoid the problem, solve the problem, or deal calmly with the worry in order to lessen the stress. Encourage the Resolver to be creative, confident, and persistent.

Direct the rest of the children to listen for workable solutions and suggestions.

Signal the two sides to begin the exchange. Coach them to play their roles enthusiastically, but don't allow them to talk over each other to the extent that no one can hear what is being said.

After a few minutes, stop the action and debrief the players and the class. Ask the Worrywarts (especially the player) if they heard any solutions or advice that could relieve the worry. If so, award a point to the Resolvers.

Continue the contest with a new pair of players and a new worry. About halfway through the allotted time, have the teams switch roles and names, so that both sides have an opportunity to offer solutions and win points.

DISCUSSION QUESTIONS

1. *How difficult was it to think of realistic solutions?*
1. *Was it easier to be a Worrywart, or a Resolver? Why?*
1. *What can you do about a worry that involves other people?*
1. *When was the last time you worried about something needlessly?*
1. *When is worry a useful emotion? When is it a waste of time? When is it destructive?*

EXERCISE AND NUTRITION

ASSESSING HEALTH HABITS

> Keeping the body healthy and balanced is an important aspect of stress management. This next series of activities provides a wide variety of experiences that give a solid grounding in healthy living.

OBJECTIVES Children will:
- Define "good health."
- Name good health habits and describe their benefits.
- Assess their own health-related behaviors.

MATERIALS One copy of the experience sheet "Health Inventory" for each child

DIRECTIONS Begin by discussing the meaning of "good health." Emphasize that good health is much more than the absence of sickness and disease. On a scale of -10 to +10, ask the children to think of being "well" (not sick) as zero, or neutral. There are many things people can do to improve their health and move up the scale, just as there are things people can do to worsen their health and move down the scale.

Ask the children to name behaviors that produce good health when they are practiced routinely. List them on the board under the heading "Good Health Habits." Include items related to diet, exercise, weight management, safety, medical care, cleanliness, sleep, stress, and attitude.

Distribute the experience sheets and go over the directions. Give the children a few minutes to complete the sheet. Ask volunteers to name the areas in which they would like to improve. Question two or three of the children about exactly what they want to achieve (e.g., lose 10 pounds, eat less junk food, jog regularly) and write corresponding goal statements on the board. Urge the children to develop plans for reaching their goals.

Finally, have the children name some of the benefits of having good health habits. Include these benefits on the list:

- More energy
- Improved concentration
- Toned, flexible muscles
- More attractive appearance
- Better complexion
- Fewer colds
- Better grades
- Feeling good

DISCUSSION QUESTIONS

1. *How do healthy habits reduce stress?*
1. *What is your favorite form of exercise?*
1. *How does exercise help maintain healthy weight?*
1. *What is your strongest health habit? How did you become strong in that area?*
1. *How could you change your school routine to make it healthier? What about your home routine?*

HEALTH INVENTORY
EXPERIENCE SHEET

Circle one number for each statement. Circle *5* if the item *describes you perfectly*, *4* if it is *mostly true*, *3* if it is *somewhat true*, *2* if it is *mostly untrue*, and *1* if it is *completely untrue*.

1. I eat at least five servings of fruits and vegetables each day. *1 2 3 4 5*
2. My weight is about right for me. *1 2 3 4 5*
3. I get at least one hour of vigorous exercise on most days. *1 2 3 4 5*
4. I have lots of energy. *1 2 3 4 5*
5. I sleep eight or more hours most nights. *1 2 3 4 5*
6. I have regular physical checkups. *1 2 3 4 5*
7. I take my time eating and enjoy meals. *1 2 3 4 5*
8. I rarely eat in fast-food restaurants. *1 2 3 4 5*
9. I believe good health is important. *1 2 3 4 5*
10. I am rarely sick. *1 2 3 4 5*
11. I wear my seatbelt when traveling in a vehicle. *1 2 3 4 5*
12. I obey safety rules and laws. *1 2 3 4 5*
13. I prefer water and juice over soft drinks and soda. *1 2 3 4 5*
14. I'd rather eat an apple than a bag of chips. *1 2 3 4 5*
15. When using a computer, I take a break every 20 minutes. *1 2 3 4 5*
16. I visit the dentist every year. *1 2 3 4 5*
17. There is someone I can talk to when I feel stressed out. *1 2 3 4 5*
18. I usually prefer doing something active rather than watching TV. *1 2 3 4 5*

Go back and review your ratings. Where can you improve? Put a check mark (✓) next to two items that you are willing to work on. Make those your health goals. If you need help writing a goal statement for each one, ask your teacher, counselor, or parent.

RATING PHYSICAL FITNESS

OBJECTIVES Children will:
- Assess their levels of physical fitness and regular activity.
- Identify obstacles to daily exercise.
- Use a problem-solving process to eliminate obstacles in sample situations.

MATERIALS One copy of the experience sheet "Getting Physical" for each child

DIRECTIONS Distribute the experience sheets and give the children a few minutes to answer the questions.

Ask volunteers to share their answers to the first two questions on the inventory. Draw parallels between activities they enjoyed as small children and those they enjoy now. Ask the children to describe the benefits of their current physical activities. Include social, leadership, and self-esteem benefits as well as physical and health benefits.

Point out that the U.S. Surgeon General has stated that children should engage in at least one hour of vigorous physical activity daily. Ask for a show of hands from children who are able to achieve this standard.

Ask the other children to name things that prevent them from getting enough exercise. Is it lack of interest? Lack of time? Lack of equipment? Lack of parental cooperation? Lack of friends to exercise with? Lack of opportunities? Write their answers on the board under the heading "Obstacles."

Take a few minutes to examine one or two of the obstacles in more detail. Once you have clearly defined each problem, brainstorm possible solutions and write them on the board. Encourage the children to be creative in their approach to solving the problems. Urge all of the children to proactively seek solutions to problems that interfere with their getting adequate exercise.

DISCUSSION QUESTIONS

1. *What physical activities do your parents pursue?*
2. *What activities do you do as a family?*
3. *Why is it helpful to vary your exercise routine?*
4. *What are some physical activities that don't require equipment?*
5. *Do kids play spontaneous pickup games in your school or neighborhood? How would you go about joining one?*

GETTING PHYSICAL
EXPERIENCE SHEET

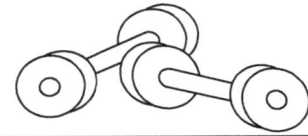

To some kids, physical education is the best thing about school. They love to be outside—moving, playing, competing, winning, even losing. It's all fun. Other kids dread physical education. To them, it's the worst thing about school, and they will do almost anything to avoid it. What about you?

1. What physical activities did you enjoy when you were a little kid? _____

2. What is your favorite sport or physical activity now? _____

3. Which sports or physical activities do you dislike? Why? _____

4. How much time do you spend exercising each day? _____

5. If you exercise less than one hour a day, what prevents you from doing more?

6. On a scale of 1 to 10, with 10 being "highly fit," how do you rate your physical fitness? _____

7. What is one thing you can do to improve your physical fitness? _____

REACH FOR THE BEST

OBJECTIVES   Children will:
- Reduce stress with easy stretching and visualization.

MATERIALS   Optional light music conducive to slow, rhythmic stretching

DIRECTIONS   Tell the children that you will read a script that involves both stretching and visualizing, and that you would like them to follow along and do what you are suggesting. Ask the children to stand in a comfortable position where they will not bump into desks, chairs, or one another. Start the music (optional) and slowly read from the script, pausing briefly between instructions.

Stand comfortably, with your feet approximately shoulder-width apart. Imagine that you are in a beautiful fruit orchard ... There are many, many fruit trees here. In front of you is a tree with your very favorite fruit ... Slowly reach up with one arm and stretch as far as you can to reach a piece of the fruit ... Lift your opposite heel off the ground as you are stretching ... Pretend you are reaching for a plump, ripe, juicy orange, apple, peach, or other fruit ... Now, reach with your other arm to pick another piece of fruit that is just a bit farther away, so you must really stretch ... As you are stretching, lift your opposing heel off the ground. This gives you just enough lift to reach that luscious piece of your favorite fruit ... Gently and slowly take those pieces of fruit and lay them on the ground in front of you, flexing your knees slightly as you bend ... Reach and pick again. This time stretch even further to get the best looking piece of fruit ... Shift your reaching from arm to arm, always lifting the opposite heel while keeping your toe on the ground ... After every few reaches, lay the fruit on the ground ... Now, pick up a piece of your favorite fruit and take a big bite ...

Enjoy the taste. It is sweet and juicy and good for your body ... As you eat the fruit, say to yourself, "I feel so good" ... "This fruit is good for me" ... "I love to eat foods that are healthy" ... After you have picked one more beautiful pieces of fruit, stretching as far as you possibly can, pick up your fruit and take it with you to your seat.

DISCUSSION QUESTIONS

1. *How did it feel to stretch your body?*
1. *Stretching builds flexibility. Why is flexibility important?*
1. *What kind of fruit were you "picking?" How did it "taste?"*
1. *Did visualizing the orchard make the stretching more fun? How?*

PYRAMID MENU PLANNING

OBJECTIVES Children will:
- ❤ Explain the organization and meaning of the Healthy Eating Pyramid.
- ❤ Assign foods eaten to locations on the pyramid and evaluate the results.
- ❤ Use the pyramid to plan meals and snacks for one day.

MATERIALS One copy of the "Healthy Eating Pyramid" experience sheet for each child; one copy of the "Menu Planning" experience sheet for each child

DIRECTIONS Begin by asking the children what they have eaten so far today. List both foods and beverages on the board. Get as much input as you can, recording duplications as check marks after various items.

Distribute the "Healthy Eating Pyramid" experience sheets. Either draw a simplified pyramid on the board or project the graphic onto the board.

Starting at the bottom of the pyramid (the foundation of exercise and weight control) discuss the various categories and the implications of their size and placement. A strength of this pyramid is that it does not dictate the number of portions in any category, but conveys relative amounts graphically. For example, it's easy to see that fruits/vegetables and whole grains are equal in size and are the most important categories.

Go through the list on the board and ask the children to decide in which category each item belongs. Using the graphic on the board, run tallies next to each category. When you have finished, let the children interpret the results. Ask volunteers to explain what the tallies say about the eating behavior of the class so far that day.

Distribute the "Menu Planning" experience sheets. Working in pairs, have the children develop menus that follow the pyramid guidelines. Circulate and offer assistance, as needed. When the children have finished their menus, ask volunteers to describe meals from their plans and explain how they comply with the pyramid. Facilitate discussion.

DISCUSSION QUESTIONS

1. *Why is exercise part of the pyramid's foundation?*
2. *What are your favorite vegetables? What's a veggie you've never tried?*
3. *What are good fats?*
4. *What are the next largest categories after vegetables/fruits and whole grains?*
5. *Which does the guide tell you to eat more of, fish or hot dogs? Why?*
6. *What was the hardest thing about planning menus that follow the pyramid?*
7. *In order to follow the pyramid, how do you need to change your eating habits?*

HEALTHY EATING PYRAMID
EXPERIENCE SHEET

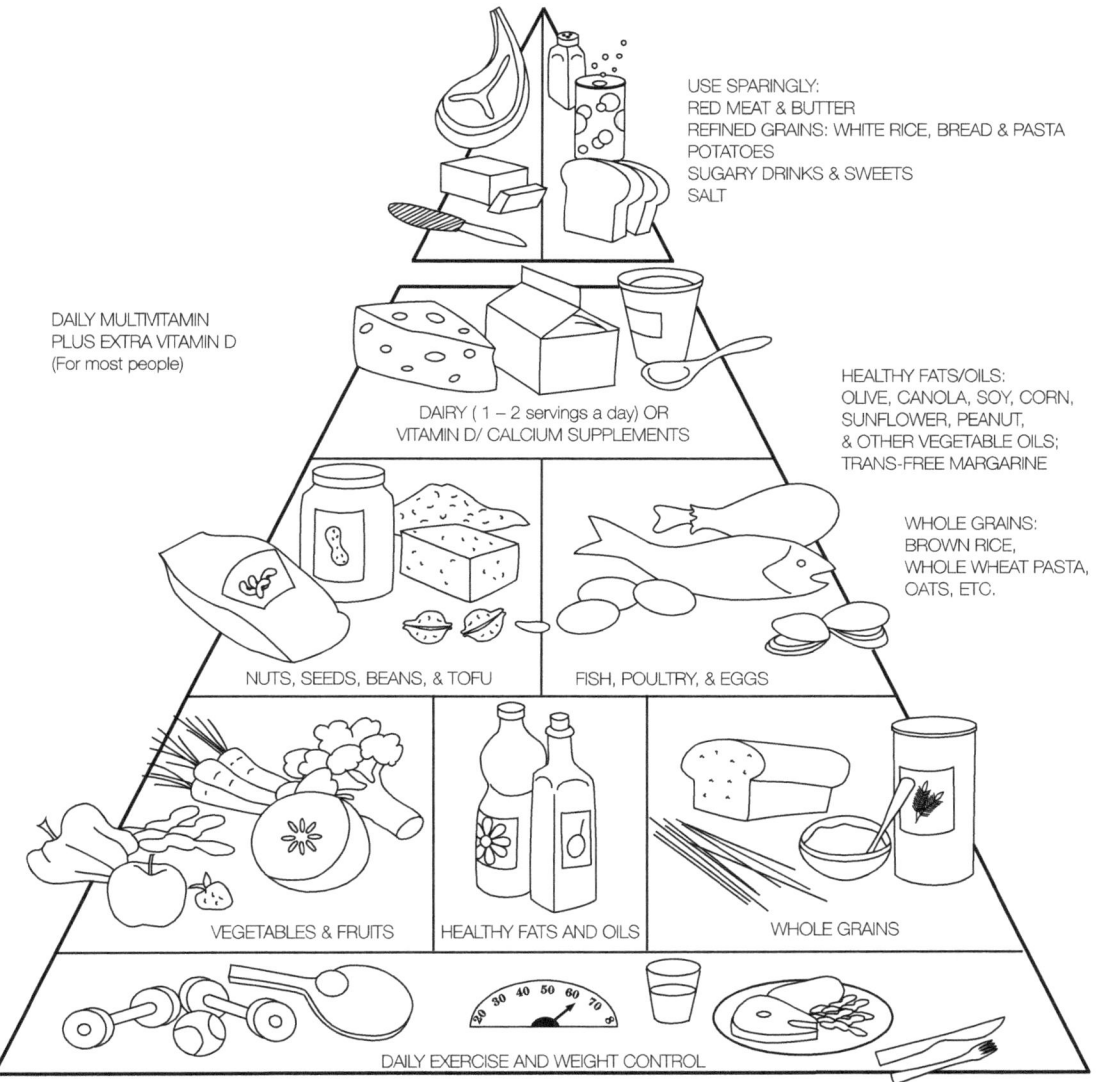

Remember:
1. Get lots of exercise.
2. Learn to love fruits and vegetables.
3. Eat whole-grain cereals and breads.
4. Nuts and seeds are great in small amounts.
5. Choose fish over meat.
6. Eat low or no-fat dairy products.
7. Cut down on sugar, salt, red meat and most baked goods.

Copyright © 2008. For more information about The Healthy Eating Pyramid, please see The Nutrition Source, Department of Nutrition, Harvard School of Public Health, http://www.thenutritionsource.org, and *Eat, Drink, and Be Healthy*, by Walter C. Willett, M.D. and Patrick J. Skerrett (2005), Free Press/Simon & Schuster Inc.

MENU PLANNING
EXPERIENCE SHEET

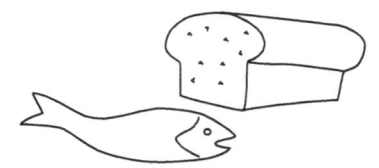

Plan all of your meals and snacks for one day. Include appropriate amounts from different levels of the Healthy Eating Pyramid. Do the best you can to make your menu match the pyramid.

BREAKFAST

SNACK

LUNCH

SNACK

DINNER

SNACK

THE BREAKFAST BOOST

OBJECTIVES Children will:

- Describe the benefits of eating breakfast.
- Develop breakfast ideas that fit the Healthy Eating Pyramid.

MATERIALS One copy of the experience sheet "The Breakfast Pyramid" for each child

DIRECTIONS Ask for a show of hands from children who ate breakfast today. Invite several of the responders to describe what they had to eat. Encourage the class to comment by asking questions, such as, "Was that a healthy breakfast?" "What was the healthiest thing about that breakfast?" and "How could you change that breakfast to make it more nutritious?"

Discuss the benefits of eating a healthy breakfast. Involve the children as much as possible. For example, if you have children who eat breakfast some mornings, but not others, ask them to describe any differences between the way they feel with and without breakfast. Point out that, in general, children who eat breakfast:

- Perform better in school.
- Get higher grades on tests.
- Have more energy for sports and other activities.
- Eat less for lunch (good for weight control).
- Don't have as many behavior problems as kids who don't eat breakfast.

Ask the children to name foods that can be part of a nutritious breakfast. Among traditional breakfast foods, include fruit, cereals, egg dishes, toast, juice, and milk. Encourage children to name nontraditional foods that could be eaten for breakfast as well. Don't be afraid to get creative.

Distribute the experience sheets. Working in pairs, have the children illustrate their blank Healthy Eating Pyramids with drawings of foods that make up healthy breakfasts. Have them display their finished pyramids and briefly discuss each one. If you like, have the class vote for the "tastiest," "healthiest," and "most unusual."

DISCUSSION QUESTIONS

1. *What healthy foods did you include in your breakfast?*
1. *In how many parts of the pyramid did you have foods?*
1. *How can breakfast help you do better in school?*
1. *What is something nutritious that you can eat when you are in a hurry?*
1. *What kinds of bread make the most nutritious toast?*

THE BREAKFAST PYRAMID
EXPERIENCE SHEET

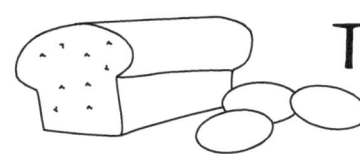

DIRECTIONS:

1. Working with your partner, come up with ideas for a healthy breakfast.
2. Decide where each food goes on the pyramid. Include every part of the meal.
3. Draw a picture of the food in the appropriate section.

Copyright © Innerchoice Publishing

SNACKING WISELY

OBJECTIVES Children will:
- Explain the benefits of healthy snacking.
- Brainstorm nutritious snack foods.
- Develop snack menus for one week.

MATERIALS One copy of the experience sheet "Snack Attack" for each child

DIRECTIONS Explain to the children that since snacking often occurs spontaneously, it is important to think ahead and prepare to satisfy sudden hunger pangs with healthy snacks. Otherwise, old habits take over, like reaching for a bag of salty chips, or grabbing a candy bar.

If the children completed the menu-planning activity, remind them that snacks were planned right along with regular meals. Explain:

Snacking between meals is not a bad thing. In fact, it is often essential for maintaining energy levels when meals are more than four or five hours apart. Snacking gets a bad rap because snack foods are often high in calories and salt and low in nutrients. When you fill up on unhealthy snacks and then skip balanced meals, you do yourself no favors. But when you eat nutritious, relatively low-calorie snacks, you benefit from the energy boost without spoiling your appetite for the next regular meal. And you don't have to worry about gaining excess weight.

Ask the children to help you brainstorm a list of nutritious snacks. Write suggestions on the board. List all suggestions. Examples: plain popcorn, whole-grain crackers with peanut butter, unsweetened fruit juices, fresh fruits and vegetables, low-fat yogurt and cheese, raisins and other dried fruit, unsalted nuts and seeds.

After brainstorming, go back over the final list and talk about questionable items, particularly snacks that might contain large amounts of sugar, salt, or fat. For example, a typical bakery muffin is made with white flour (not whole grain), is high in sugar, and may contain trans fats, which are even worse for the heart and blood vessels than saturated fats, such as butter and lard. After discussing an unhealthy snack, cross it off the list.

If computers are available, ask teams of children to research the "bad" ingredients that you have been urging them to avoid. Have them read and report on the effects of sugar, salt, saturated fats, and trans fats on the body.

Distribute the experience sheets and discuss the assignment. Encourage the children to be specific when making their choices. For example, instead of listing "fruit" as a snack, they should describe the type and amount of fruit, such as "1 apple," or "large bunch of grapes."

DISCUSSION QUESTIONS

1. *Ask volunteers to read their snack lists to the class. Facilitate discussion.*
1. *What kinds of snacks are available from most vending machines?*
1. *Where can you find healthy snacks?*
1. *What kinds of snack foods does your family keep at home?*
1. *What can you do to improve your own snacking habits?*

SNACK ATTACK
EXPERIENCE SHEET

PLAN NUTRITIOUS SNACKS FOR FIVE DAYS.

Monday
- Midmorning _____
- Afternoon _____
- Evening _____

Tuesday
- Midmorning _____
- Afternoon _____
- Evening _____

Wednesday
- Midmorning _____
- Afternoon _____
- Evening _____

Thursday
- Midmorning _____
- Afternoon _____
- Evening _____

Friday
- Midmorning _____
- Afternoon _____
- Evening _____

If your heart is in Social-Emotional Learning, visit us online.

Come see us at
www.InnerchoicePublishing.com

Our web site gives you a look at all our other Social-Emotional Learning-based books, free activities, articles, research, and learning and teaching strategies. Every week you'll get a new Sharing Circle topic and lesson.

INNERCHOICE Publishing
15079 Oak Chase Court
Wellington, FL 33414